Politics as Leadership

The Paul Anthony Brick Lectures

Eleventh Series

Politics
as Leadership

Robert C. Tucker

University of Missouri Press
Columbia & London
1981

University of Missouri Press, Columbia, Missouri 65211
Library of Congress Catalog Card Number 81–1982
Printed and bound in the United States of America

Library of Congress Cataloging in Publication Data

    Tucker, Robert C.
      Politics as Leadership.

      (The Paul Anthony Brick lectures; 11th ser.)
      1. Leadership. 2. Authority. 3. Power
(Social sciences) I. Title. II. Series: Paul
Anthony Brick lectures; 11th ser.
    HM141.T83   303.3'4   81–1982
    ISBN 0–8262–0341–8   AACR2

In Memoriam

Adele Steinfels Tucker

1891–1972

Preface

Most students of politics, myself included, have specialized interests. Mine lie largely in the history and politics of Russia. But for many years I have been intrigued by a fundamental question of universal bearing: What *is* politics?

The extended answer that gradually took shape in my mind through reading, observation, and reflection is presented in broad contours in this book. Its thesis is that politics in its essential nature is leadership of a political community and all the activity, including participatory activity by citizens, that may enter into the process of leadership. The first three chapters give an analytic account of politics in leadership terms. The final chapter is an experiment in applied leadership analysis, an attempt to show how the principles enunciated in the earlier chapters can illuminate what leadership might mean in the world situation of our troubled time.

In this final chapter, the study departs the ground of dispassionate theoretical analysis to take a stand on problems of supreme concern. It seeks to convey a sense of the desperate need for historically unprecedented forms of leadership in order to prevent the human venture from ending in shipwreck. It addresses the question of what political leadership means for governments and movements alive to the range of challenges that imperil civilization now.

This book developed from the Paul Anthony Brick lectures given at the University of Missouri in the spring of 1980. My thanks go to Professor Joseph Bien, Chairman of the Brick Lectures Committee, his fellow Committee members, and many others at the University for warm hospitality and the stimulating discussions that accompanied the lectures. Being myself a native Missourian, I found it especially meaningful to return home for this purpose.

I am grateful to several colleagues and friends who kindly read the book in manuscript and shared with me their reactions: professors Robert W. Adamson, Cyril E. Black, Michael R. Curtis, W. Philip Davison, and Richard A. Falk, Mrs. Reiko Lih, Mr. George Brockway, and Mr. James L. Mairs. Their comments have been most helpful to me in the final editing. Responsibility for remaining deficiencies is mine.

R. C. T.
Princeton, N. J.
March 1981

Contents

To be rational is to think; and for a man who proposes to act, the thing that it is important to think about is the situation in which he stands. . . . Whether his action is to prove successful or not depends on whether he grasps the situation rightly or not. If he is a wise man, it is not until he has consulted his oracle, done everything in his power to find out what the situation is, that he will make even the most trivial plan. And if he neglects the situation, the situation will not neglect him. It is not one of those gods that leave an insult unpunished.

R. G. Collingwood, *The Idea of History*

. . . we have become a species mortally dangerous to itself.

Erik Erikson, *Dimensions of a New Identity*

1

The Essence of Politics: Two Views

Systematic thought about politics began in Greece about two and a half millenia ago, and an academic discipline called *political science* has flourished in various countries for a century or so. Yet there is still no consensus on the essential nature of the discipline's subject. Political scientists are not in general agreement about what it is they are studying. Let us then begin at the beginning: What is politics?

There is a classic answer to this question, and likewise a classic dissent. Both appear in the Platonic dialogues. The answer, advocated in the dialogues by the Sophists, holds that politics is in essence the pursuit and exercise of power—in the interest of those who pursue and exercise it. As Gorgias the rhetorician expounds this position in Plato's dialogue the *Gorgias*, the chief good in human life is power, and statesmen acquire power through the art of persuasion, rhetoric. So, for example, Pericles owed his power over the Athenian city-state to his command of persuasive eloquence. The same theme is argued by another character in the dialogue, Callicles, in a starker way. He declares it a natural law ("Nature's *nomos*") that those with greater power rule the polis for self-seeking purposes, imposing their will upon the weak. Callicles, it has been observed, was propounding, long in advance, Nietzsche's idea of the superman imbued with *Wille zur Macht*.[1]

1. A. E. Taylor, *Plato: The Man and His Work* (New York: The Dial Press, 1936), p. 119.

1

Plato makes Socrates the exponent of the dissenting view. Socrates does not deny the factual prevalence of politics as the self-interested rule of the powerful in most times and places. But this merely means that true statesmanship (*politiké*) is a rare phenomenon on earth. Indeed, Socrates says in one place: "I think that I am the only or almost the only Athenian who practices the true art of politics; I am the only politician of my time."[2] The idea underlying this statement is that statesmanship is an art analogous to gymnastics and medicine, arts that tend to the body. Just as medicine is the art of tending the body with a view to restoring it to a healthy state, so statesmanship is tendance of the soul, whether through legislation, which establishes a standard of the soul's health, or through the administration of justice, which cures diseases of the soul. Rhetoric, the art of persuasion, is sham politics, rather as cosmetics, the artful decking out of the body, are sham gymnastics. The true statesman, possessing knowledge of what is good for man, is a physician of souls. So runs Plato's argument in the *Gorgias*. Elsewhere, as in the late dialogue the *Politicus*, he varies the analogy and pictures the statesman as shepherd of the human flock. Statesmanship is the art of tending the flock.

I think it fair to characterize Plato's dissenting view as one that equates politics with leadership. He does not deny that rulers exercise power, whether in accordance with law as in the case of the righteous king or arbitrarily and autocratically as in the case of the tyrant. But he believes that in essence, ideally, politics has a positive function to perform for the community of citizens in which the ruler exercises power. It is not the exercise of power for power's sake, nor is it the simulacrum of statesmanship

2. *Gorgias*, in *The Dialogues of Plato*, trans. B. Jowett, 2 vols. (New York: Random House, 1937), 1: 582.

that the rhetorician may produce by flattering the populace with his art of persuasion. It is an activity with utility for the polis, the activity of giving direction to the community of citizens in the management of their common affairs, especially with a view to the training and improvement of their souls. The notion of politics as the directive function in the state is the crux of Plato's position. In our time we can hardly rest content with his further thought that the directive function consists in the moral tendance of citizens' souls. Still, his great achievement was to formulate, or at any rate to adumbrate, a leadership approach to the nature of politics as distinct from the power approach that was widely accepted in his time and is still widely accepted in ours.

The position taken in these pages is in the Platonic tradition. While recognizing, as any realistic view must, that power considerations bulk very large in political life, it holds that politics in essence is leadership, or attempted leadership, of whatever is the prevailing form of political community. It departs from Plato in advancing this as a descriptive proposition rather than a normative one. Leadership is not an ideal form of political rule; it is what we factually find when we study closely the political process. Consequently, in what follows we shall analyze leadership as a value-neutral phenomenon. We shall see that political leadership comes in many forms: effective and ineffective; wise, constructive, and beneficial to the political community on some occasions, and unwise, destructive, and disastrous on others. We shall also take into account the relativity of leadership in that what may be effective or advantageous leadership for one political community may, by that very token, be disadvantageous for another that is at cross-purposes with the first. The problem of moral evaluation of political leadership will, however, arise for us at various points in the study.

3

The Power School

In modern times, the classic answer has generally prevailed over the recurring dissent. From Machiavelli, who produced in *The Prince* a "how-to" manual for the princely power-seeker and power-holder, the concept of politics as power has been a salient strain in political theorizing. In the nineteenth and twentieth centuries it has been, I believe, the dominant school.

Machiavelli's advice to the prince leaves us in no doubt as to what, in the Florentine's view, politics is about. After considering the various kinds of government, he raises the key issues, such as: The Way to Govern Cities or Dominions That, Previous to Being Occupied, Lived Under Their Own Laws; Of New Dominions Which Have Been Acquired by One's Own Arms and Ability; Of Those Who Have Attained the Position of Prince by Villainy; How the Strength of All States Should Be Measured; Of Cruelty and Clemency, and Whether It Is Better to Be Loved or Feared; Whether Fortresses and Other Things Which Princes Often Contrive Are Useful or Injurious; and How a Prince Must Act in Order to Gain Reputation.

Marx, like his master Hegel, was an admiring reader of Machiavelli and may have been especially struck by the statement in chapter nine of *The Prince* that there are "two opposite parties" in every city, "arising from the desire of the populace to avoid the oppression of the great, and the desire of the great to command and oppress the people." The "two opposite parties" resemble the two opposing classes of Marx's class-struggle doctrine. Marx views the state as an agency of the power of a possessing class and politics as the coercive use of state power to protect the possessing class's mode of production and the associated set of property relations. Consistent with this position, revolutionary politics is the deployment of rebellious coercive power to overthrow an existing state order and the socioeconomic structure that it protects. As Marx's disciple Lenin put it, the state is "a special kind of cudgel, *rien de plus*."[3]

From Marx's teaching on politics as class power the influential Italian school of politics as elite power took its rise in Gaetano Mosca and Vilfredo Pareto. The elite theorists could be described as disillusioned Marxists. Marx envisaged a human future without classes, hence without the state and the politics of power, whereas the elite theorists believe it to be written in the constitution of man and society that there will forever be a division between a power-holding minority, the ruling elite, and a majority that submits to the elite's power. The majority submits because of coercion or through acceptance of an ideological "political formula" that masks the situation of elite rule.

Academic political science in mid-twentieth-century America has been strongly under the influence of the power approach to the political process. The elite theory found a well-known application to America in C. Wright Mills's book *The Power Elite* and other works of its genre. Some theorists, perhaps best typified by Anthony Downs in *An Economic Theory of Democracy*, have sought to construct a politics on the analogy of economics. The postulated wealth-maximizing "economic man" of modern political economy finds his counterpart here in a postulated power-maximizing "political man" single-mindedly seeking to win elections and stay in office through coalition-building in party politics. In this model, the ulterior purposes for which power is desired are of no more interest to the political scientist than those for which economic man desires wealth are to the political economist.

3. V. I. Lenin, "The Dictatorship of the Proletariat," *The Lenin Anthology*, ed. Robert C. Tucker (New York: W. W. Norton, 1975), p. 490.

To other power theorists, best instanced by the late Harold Lasswell, the inner sources of the postulated power motivation are of profound importance. Having described politics in an earlier text as "the study of influence and the influential," or "who gets what, when and how," Lasswell went on, in his book *Power and Personality*, to define a political man (*homo politicus*, to use his own phrase) as one who accentuates power, demands power for the self, accentuates expectations concerning power, and acquires at least a minimum proficiency in the skills of power. This definition of political man as power-seeker was accompanied by the hypothesis that "power is expected to overcome low estimates of the self."[4] By "power" Lasswell meant the capacity of a person to dominate or determine the actions of others. In a forthright later statement of this position, he wrote: "In human affairs the demand to coerce is the phenomenon with which we are most concerned as professional students of politics."[5] Not all or even most contemporary political scientists would agree with all of these statements, but there might be something approximating a consensus on Lasswell's broader proposition, cited approvingly in a text by Robert Dahl, that politics may be defined as "the study of the shaping and sharing of power."[6]

We have touched very briefly upon some influential

4. The earlier statement appears in Harold D. Lasswell, *Politics: Who Gets What, When, How* (New York: Meridian Books, 1958), p. 7; the book was first published in 1936. The remaining citations appear in Harold D. Lasswell, *Power and Personality* (New York: W. W. Norton, 1976), pp. 39, 57, 223; this book was first published in 1948.

5. "Afterthoughts: Thirty Years Later," in Harold D. Lasswell, *Psychopathology and Politics* (New York: The Viking Press, 1960), p. 278; this book was first published in 1930.

6. Cited by Robert A. Dahl, *Modern Political Analysis* (Prentice-Hall, 1963), p. 5, from Harold D. Lasswell and Abraham Kaplan, *Power and Society* (New Haven: Yale University Press, 1950), p. xiv.

versions of the concept of politics as power-seeking. A full and systematic examination of that position is beyond the scope of our study. What can be said by way of general evaluation of it? First, it seems clear that the pursuit of power goes on constantly under all political systems of which we know. To acquire the role of a constituted political leader, in other words, to occupy an official leadership position in a political order, a person normally seeks power by whatever are the prescribed or permitted means and procedures, and once having become a constituted leader he often seeks to enhance his power position. Moreover, the student of political history is likely to find, here and there, some individuals who resemble in their behavior and motivation the power-lusting *homo politicus* that Lasswell has pictured, or the power-maximizing party politician of Downs's theory of democracy.

But all this having been acknowledged, the dissenter has some telling arguments to advance against the view that reduces politics to the seeking and exercise of power. First, some constituted leaders have shown themselves capable, at one time or another, of rising above personal or party power considerations in their political conduct. More important, some persons have been or are now political leaders without possessing power or occupying high political office; some among these have not even aspired to it. They will be called here *nonconstituted leaders*. Examples from recent history might include Mohandas Gandhi, Martin Luther King, Jr., Dr. Albert Schweitzer, Milovan Djilas, Jean Monnet, and Academician Andrei Sakharov, a nonconstituted leader of contemporary Russia who not only is without political power but at present (late 1980) is also under house arrest in the town of Gorky. In what sense or senses nonconstituted leaders may function as political leaders without possessing power remains to be explained later in our study.

Finally, and this may be the decisive point, the power approach fails to tell us what political leaders do, or are expected to do, in their capacities as leaders. To define politics as the exercise of power is rather like saying that an airplane pilot manipulates wheels and levers. He certainly does that, but he does it in the process of flying the airplane. The question that the power theorists fail to answer, or to answer satisfactorily, is: What is the equivalent of "flying the airplane" for people of power in political life? Or, to return to the economic analogy favored by political scientists like Downs, economic man maximizes his wealth in the course of providing certain goods or services. What "goods or services" does political man provide in the course of maximizing his power, or with the power that he has maximized? It is not my contention that the power approach has no great relevance to the understanding of politics, but I do think that it is critically inadequate as a basis for such understanding, because it does not reveal what it is that political leaders do or attempt to do with the power that most really do seek and some do exercise.

The power approach is not to be disposed of, however, by such considerations. One who does not accept the view that politics in its essence is the pursuit and the wielding of power must produce an explanation for the tenacity of that view through the centuries, for the fact that so many eminent thinkers, some with practical political experience, have espoused it. The political theorizing of such figures as Machiavelli, Marx, and Mosca and such political scientists of our time as Lasswell is not to be lightly dismissed on the strength of the arguments that have been adduced here.

But in order to understand why the power approach has recommended itself so strongly to so formidable a collection of minds, we must first outline an acceptable alternative to it.

The Leadership Approach

If the antecedents of the leadership approach go back to Plato, the idea of building a systematic politics upon the foundation of a concept of leadership belongs primarily to the twentieth century. Max Weber pointed the way early in the century. In his essay on "Politics as a Vocation" (1918) he defined politics as "the leadership, or the influencing of the leadership, of a *political* association, hence, today, of a *state*," and added that by a "state" he meant a "human community that (successfully) claims the *monopoly of the legitimate use of physical force* within a given territory." The conception of the state as "a relation of men dominating men" led Weber, however, to a modified version of the power theory—modified in the sense that politics as a discipline became the study of "authority" defined as legitimized domination in its various forms.[7] No systematic account of politics in terms of leadership emerged.

It is in the recent history of political science that we see the beginning of conscious efforts in this direction. Such efforts have begun, partly, in disillusion with the power approach. James MacGregor Burns, the author of a major attempt at recasting political analysis in leadership terms, formulates this feeling as a confession:

7. *From Max Weber: Essays in Sociology*, ed. H. H. Gerth and C. Wright Mills (New York: Oxford University Press, 1958), pp. 77, 78. For a proposal to construct political science as a study of authority relations, see Harry Eckstein, "Authority Patterns: A Structural Basis for Political Inquiry," *American Political Science Review* 67: 4 (December 1973): 1142–61.

As a political scientist I have belonged to a "power school" that analyzed the interrelationships of persons on the basis only of power. Perhaps this was fitting for an era of two world wars and revolutions, the unleashing of the inhuman force of the atom. I fear, however, that we are paying a steep intellectual and political price for our preoccupation with power. Viewing politics *as* power has blinded us to the crucial role of power *in* politics and hence to the pivotal role of leadership.[8]

Others might differently explain their sense of the need to take the leadership road in theorizing about politics. The significant fact is that increasing numbers of practitioners of the discipline are showing that they feel such a need. An anthology of articles on political leadership, published in 1972, was subtitled "Readings for an Emerging Field," and the editor, in a subsequent volume of his own on this subject, summed up the status of the idea of political leadership as follows: "Past neglect. Present emergence. Future potential." "Now," he went on, "we need to ask, 'What is meant by political leadership?'"[9]

He thereby called attention to the fact that leadership is an elusive phenomenon and that there is no consensus among political scientists on what it means. Others have stressed the same point. "The precise nature of political leadership is one of the most difficult problems in the domain of politics, or indeed, in social action, yet it is one of the most real phenomena in political and social behavior," wrote the eminent Chicago political scientist Charles E. Merriam in 1945.[10] "Leadership is one of the most ob-

8. James MacGregor Burns, *Leadership* (New York: Harper & Row, 1978), p. 11.
9. Glenn D. Paige, *Political Leadership: Readings for an Emerging Field* (New York: The Free Press, 1972); Glenn D. Paige, *The Scientific Study of Political Leadership* (New York: The Free Press, 1977), p. 61.
10. Charles E. Merriam, *Systematic Politics* (Chicago: University of Chicago Press, 1966), p. 107; this book was first published in 1945.

served and least understood phenomena on earth," wrote James MacGregor Burns thirty-three years later.[11] Some find the difficulty of understanding so great that further inquiry seems not worth the effort. One political scientist refers to "the disappearing act called leadership" and remarks that "all paths to the study of leadership end up by swallowing their subject matter."[12] Perhaps the great difficulty of conceptualizing leadership helps to explain why many political scientists still prefer the seemingly more manageable project of analyzing politics—and leadership itself—in power terms.

Why is it so difficult to bring the phenomenon of leadership into conceptual focus? One part of the answer is that the most readily apparent way of doing so is not, analytically, the most promising path to take. Leadership is a fact of social life in all spheres, not in politics only, and wherever found it appears under the aspect of a relationship between leaders and those whom they lead. Leadership is a process of human interaction in which some individuals exert, or attempt to exert, a determining influence upon others. This being so, it has seemed natural to proceed by inquiring into the nature of this leader–follower relationship, raising such questions as: What explains why some persons, rather than others, emerge as leaders? Who are the leaders? By what means do they achieve their leadership roles? Why do their followers accept them as leaders? What is the nature of the interaction between them? What are the different forms of the relationship between leaders and followers?

Thus, in advocating what he called a "politics by leadership conception," Lester Seligman wrote that such a conception would concern itself with generalizing con-

11. Burns, *Leadership*, p. 2.
12. Aaron Wildavsky, in *The New York Times Book Review*, 27 April 1980, p. 12.

cerning four types of relations: "(1) the relations of leaders to led within particular structures, (2) the relationship between leaders of political structures, (3) the relationship between leaders of one structure and the followers of another, and (4) the relationship between leaders and the 'unorganized' or nonaffiliated."[13] Burns, for his part, defines leadership as "leaders inducing followers to act for certain goals that represent the values and the motivations—the wants and needs, the aspirations and expectations—*of both leaders and followers*."[14] This results in the exclusion of dictators from the category of leaders. Adolf Hitler appears, in Burns's analysis, as "an absolute wielder of brutal power"[15] and, as such, *not* a leader. Although such a line of reasoning reflects our feeling that leadership involves a voluntary response of followers to leaders, it gives rise to serious problems of political analysis. First, we have much evidence that dictators, including such archetypal twentieth-century ones as Hitler and Stalin, had very many willing followers in their time, the first especially in his earlier years of rule in Germany, and the second especially in his war leadership of Russia in 1941–1945. Second, Burns's view bypasses the key question of what it is that leaders do, or how they function as leaders, apart from interacting motivationally with followers. Hence he is blocked off from allowing that the leader–follower relationship covers a wide spectrum, ranging from dictatorial forms of leadership at one extreme to highly participatory or democratic forms at the other. A leadership approach to politics must not rule out by its terms of reference the phenomenon of authoritarian or dictatorial leadership. That Hitler and Stalin were po-

13. Lester G. Seligman, "The Study of Political Leadership," *American Political Science Review* 44: 4 (December 1950): 914.
14. Burns, *Leadership*, p. 19.
15. Ibid., p. 27.

litical leaders is no less a fact than that they were absolute wielders of brutal power.

The upshot is that while leadership is unquestionably a relation between leaders and followers in interaction and may for various purposes be analyzed as such, a theory of political leadership cannot easily be developed by elaborating the relational aspect. The more fruitful way is to start with the question of what it is that leaders do, or try to do, in their capacities as leaders, what functions do they perform in the process of exerting influence upon their followers? Here I repeat the point already made in my discussion of the power school, namely, that as political scientists we must specify what sorts of "goods or services" leaders provide in the exercise of political power.

In proceeding along this line, a political scientist is well advised to consider the contributions of a sister discipline. If students of politics have been deficient in the study of leadership until recently, the same cannot be said of social psychologists. A survey of twentieth-century research on leadership in social psychology devotes a quarter of its six hundred pages to bibliography alone.[16] The social psychologists have proceeded largely by working with small experimental groups, observing who in a particular group emerges as a leader, and seeking to identify the attributes of this person, or of this person in conjunction with the group's situation, that account for the result.

In *Heroes and Hero-Worship and the Heroic in History* (1841), Thomas Carlyle proposed that there are certain individuals whose innate superiority along one or another line stamps them as natural leaders. Among twentieth-century social psychologists, this became

16. Ralph M. Stogdill, *Handbook of Leadership: A Survey of Theory and Research* (New York: The Free Press, 1974).

13

known as the "great-man" theory of leadership. Experimental research did not bear it out. It seemed, rather, that the nature of the group's situation determined who of its members would emerge as a group leader. If the group was in a fighting situation, then someone with martial capability would; if it was in a situation that called for careful planning, then someone with the qualities of a planner would; and so on. Eventually this extreme "situationist" perspective was abandoned in favor of a middle position that recognizes the existence of certain general leadership qualities—intelligence, alertness to the needs and motives of others, insight into situations, initiative, persistence, and self-confidence—along with the variability of leadership traits according to the demands of group situations.[17] More important than that conclusion, however, is an insight that resulted from research on leaders' attributes, namely, that "leadership flourishes only in a problem situation."[18]

Because the social psychologists frequently work with small experimental groups and can arrange the situations in which leadership emerges, they have tended to assume that the nature of the problem situation is a "given," self-evident to the group's members. But would this be true in real-life situations involving large groups, particularly those in political life? Might it not very often be the case in politics that the problem needs to be specified, the situation interpreted or defined, and that just this is one of the functions that leadership serves, perhaps the prime function? With that crucial critical reservation

17. Ibid., chap. 6; and R. M. Stogdill, "Personal Factors Associated with Leadership," in *Leadership*, ed. C. A. Gibb (Middlesex, Eng.: Penguin Books, 1969), p. 127.

18. C. A. Gibb, "The Principles and Traits of Leadership," in *Leadership*, ed. Gibb, p. 211.

14

in mind, I will steer in what follows by the lodestar of Gibb's proposition that leadership flourishes in problem situations.

Leadership as Activity

Let us begin with Plato's view that leadership has a directive function. A leader is one who gives direction to a collective's activities. The collective may be of any size or kind. It may be a small informal group such as a gang of hoodlums. It may be a university, a business corporation, or an army. In these cases we are dealing with criminal, business, educational, and military leadership respectively. If the group in question is a political community, whether a municipality, a province, a nation-state, or an international organization, then we are speaking of political leadership. A political leader is one who gives direction, or meaningfully participates in the giving of direction, to the activities of a political community.

The idea of leadership's directive function is supported by a kind of imagery that leaders in different times and cultures have frequently used in addressing their followers or those who they hoped would become their followers. It is the imagery of the journey or the road, of direction-giving in a literal sense. The leader will say that the group, or the society, is traveling along a certain path but ought to take a different one, or that the group stands at a crossroads beyond which stretch two alternative roads: one that will lead to the desired destination and another that will lead only to grief and trouble. We shall encounter this metaphor more than once in statements of political leaders who will be cited below.

If political and other groups are in need of direction, this must be because of uncertainty about what courses of collective action are desirable. One might argue that even in ordinary, day-to-day group life, when no great uncertainties exist, groups are in need of being directed. But such routine direction might better be described as *management*, reserving the term *leadership* for the directing of a group at times of choice, change, and decision, times when deliberation and authoritative decision occur, followed by steps to implement decisions reached. In more familiar terms directly applicable to political leadership, political communities confront situations in which policy must be formulated, promulgated, and executed.

To clarify what is meant by a *situation* (which will be used here as synonymous with *problem situation*), imagine that you are on holiday and visiting a foreign city for the first time. One day you leave your hotel in mid-afternoon to go for a walk. You drift along enjoying the scene. You walk by a river, through a park, and along winding streets. There *is* no situation, only a set of pleasant circumstances, so pleasant in fact that you take no notice of the passage of time. Then, as the sun starts to set, you suddenly recall that you are to meet a friend at your hotel at seven and go to dinner. You look at your watch and see that the time is already 6:45. You say to yourself: "I'm lost and I'm going to be late!" Now you are in a situation, and these words are your diagnosis, your definition, of it. You think of various possible courses of action that might be taken in the situation. You can hail a taxi, try to find a bus going in the direction of the hotel, or phone your friend and change the time of meeting. You choose what seems the best way out, and act accordingly.

Generalizing, we may say that a situation is a set of circumstances that someone endows with meaning because of the way in which they relate to that person's purposes and concerns. In the hypothetical case just mentioned, the circumstances were the distance from the hotel, the ignorance of the way back, and the seven o'clock date; the purpose that caused them to be endowed with meaning was the intention to keep the date. Situations are thus both objective and subjective in character. The circumstances, although they may be misread or incompletely known, are objective facts; they are whatever they are. The meaning with which they are endowed, however, turns on the purposes and concerns of the people involved; it is inescapably subjective. The interpreting of the meaning is, moreover, a mental act. Finally, situations are practical in that circumstances are endowed with meaning in such a way that some action is required in order to meet them.

The gist of this was said long ago by the American sociologist W. I. Thomas. Prior to any self-determined act, he wrote, there is always a stage of examination and deliberation that may be called the "defining of the situation." To drive the point home dramatically, Thomas would cite the case of a person who was institutionalized in New York State after several episodes in which he shot strangers passing on the street. In each instance the stranger's lips were moving and the man imagined that he was being called vile names. Having thus endowed the circumstances of the moving lips with dire meaning for himself, he responded murderously. Thomas drew the conclusion as follows:

> If men define those situations as real, they are real in their consequences. The total situation will always contain more or less subjective factors, and the behavior reactions can be studied only in connection with the whole context, that is, the situation as it exists in verifiable, objective terms, and as it has seemed to exist in terms of the interested person.[19]

19. W. I. Thomas, "The Relation of Research to the Social Process,"

The proposition, "If men define those situations as real, they are real in their consequences," is known as the Thomas theorem. We shall see its importance as an underlying premise in the study of political leadership.

When an individual defines a situation on his own and acts in it, leadership as an influencing relationship is not involved (except insofar as we wish to consider that each person exercises leadership of himself in life situations as they occur—an idea in the tradition of Plato). The functional need for leadership arises when people form groups for purposive action, and it arises in the group context because of the necessity of coordinated action when circumstances are endowed with meaning in such a way that a *group situation* is defined and action by the group, or on its behalf, takes place. When groups are small, leadership may be informal and shift from one element or individual in the group to another depending upon the character of the situations encountered. When groups are large and organized, there is usually a formal leadership structure. Examples are the high command of an army, the management of a corporation, the officials of a trade union, or the administration of a university. The leadership structure of a political community is its government.

We may divide leadership's directive function into three phases, although it will become evident further on that in practice these phases are interpenetrating. First, leadership has a diagnostic function. Leaders are expected to define the situation authoritatively for the group. Second, they must prescribe a course of group action, or of action on the group's behalf, that will meet the situation as defined. They must formulate a plan of action designed to resolve the problem in a manner that will serve

in *W. I. Thomas on Social Organization and Social Personality*, ed. Morris Janowitz (Chicago: University of Chicago Press, 1966), p. 301.

group purposes. These, of course, may in practice be the purposes of some particular element of the group that equates its own aims with those of the group as a whole. Third, leadership has a mobilizing function. Leaders must gain the group's support, or predominant support, for the definition of the group situation that they have advanced and for the plan of action that they have prescribed. We may describe these functions as diagnostic, policy formulating, and policy implementing.

Two familiar historical examples, both involving leadership in international politics, may be cited for purposes of illustration. The circumstances in the first can be stated quite briefly. On 7 December 1941 the Japanese air force carried out a surprise attack and sank most of the U.S. Pacific fleet, which was lying at anchor at Pearl Harbor in Hawaii. The next day Pres. Franklin D. Roosevelt went before Congress, reported these circumstances, plus the further circumstance that the German and Italian governments had declared war on the United States, and defined the situation for the American political community: the nation was at war. The president said in his speech that 7 December 1941 was "a day that will live in infamy." He prescribed a policy response, calling upon Congress to declare war upon Japan, Germany, and Italy. It promptly did so. The entire session lasted, perhaps, no more than forty-five minutes. The meaning that the reported circumstances had for the United States, their impingement upon the country's purposes and concerns, was immediately clear: the country was in danger, it was in a war situation. In this instance, the mobilization of public support for the proposed policy response presented no difficulty. Mobilization meant just that—mobilization for war. Since the nature of the situation and the necessity of the military response were clear to all, the country rapidly mobilized for the long hard war that lay ahead.

The other case occurred in Europe in 1938. It came about as a result of one of a series of aggressive steps taken by Adolf Hitler after he became leader of Germany. Not long after annexing Austria to Germany in early 1938, Hitler started to make menacing noises toward Czechoslovakia. His pretext was that ethnic Germans in a border area of the Czechoslovak republic, the Sudetenland, were being mistreated. Although a small country, Czechoslovakia was then a considerable military power, with a one-and-a-half-million-strong army deployed along a powerful fortified line of defense in hilly terrain and a well-developed defense industry. The peoples of this country had a strong will to defend its independence. It was estimated that even fighting all alone against Germany's army of that time, Czechoslovakia could hold out for three months. Furthermore, she had a treaty of alliance with France, then the strongest land power in Europe, and France was allied with Great Britain, the strongest naval power. Germany was rearming, but this process was not complete and the Nazi army was not yet up to planned strength.

Hitler's threats and bluster raised the specter of conflict. The circumstances were endowed with grim meaning by the French and the British as well as by the Czechs themselves and the German people. There was the possibility of a new European war involving the fates of all these countries and others as well. From May 1938, and especially from August, when Hitler issued an ultimatum on the Sudeten question, the existence of a most serious problem situation was accepted by all. There was no doubt among the allies that it was a situation of danger. But along with agreement on that main point, there were important differences among different leaders' diagnoses of the danger and their prescriptions for policy response. There were differences, too, on the German side.

Twenty years earlier, France and Britain had endured a terrible war with Germany. Public opinion in both countries was strongly in favor of preserving peace if at all possible. This concern was on the minds of the constituted leaders of the two governments, Prime Minister Neville Chamberlain of Britain and Premier Édouard Daladier of France, and it was not lost on the minds of others in responsible positions. Under the influence, in part, of the peace-at-almost-any-price sentiment, Chamberlain and Daladier decided to seek a way out by negotiating with Hitler, and they chose to take him at his word when he claimed that his concern was the fate of the Sudeten Germans. As they defined the problem situation, it was one of local conflict that could be regulated by the major powers given a modicum of goodwill and flexibility on all sides.

Winston Churchill and some others, including First Lord of the Admiralty Duff Cooper, diagnosed the situation differently. As they saw it, there was a discrepancy between Hitler's public definition of the situation as one of local conflict over the Sudetenland and his private definition, in other words, his actual diagnosis, of it. In their opinion, Hitler had diagnosed the situation as an opportunity to destroy Czechoslovakia as a major obstacle on his march to mastery of Europe, and he wanted to accomplish this with the help of Britain and France by persuading their fearful leaders to pressure Pres. Eduard Beneš of Czechoslovakia into submission to the demand for cession of the Sudetenland to Germany. To Churchill and Duff Cooper, therefore, the situation was not simply that peace was in danger, but that the democratic states were in mortal danger if Hitler succeeded in swallowing up Czechoslovakia. That would gravely weaken the Allies' military position and correspondingly strengthen Hitler's. Consequently, they favored a different policy response from the one that Chamberlain and Daladier were proposing. While not declaring war, they would be supportive of the Czechs and thereby show Hitler that Britain and France were prepared, *if necessary*, to go to war in order to prevent Czechoslovakia from being overrun. In that case, they reasoned, he would draw back.[20]

These varying diagnoses of the danger differed decisively in the interpretation of Hitler's mind and motives. No one could be certain about those things, yet any diagnosis of the situation had to be based upon some assessment of them. When Duff Cooper made his eloquent resignation speech at the opening of the subsequent three-day debate on the Munich crisis in the House of Commons, he particularly stressed the difference over the interpretation of Hitler's mind by saying:

> The Prime Minister has confidence in the good will and in the word of Herr Hitler, although, when Herr Hitler broke the Treaty of Versailles, he undertook to keep the Treaty of Locarno, and when he broke the Treaty of Locarno, he undertook not to interfere further, or to have further territorial claims in Europe. When he entered Austria by force, he authorized his henchmen to give an authoritative assurance that he would not interfere with Czechoslovakia. That was less than six months ago. Still the Prime Minister believes that he can rely upon the good faith of Hitler.[21]

The rest, of course, is familiar history. Chamberlain and Daladier made a deal with Hitler in Munich and prevailed on Beneš to accept it. Hitler proceeded to dismember Czechoslovakia in stages, as Churchill and Duff Cooper had thought he would do, and the Second World

20. My account of the Munich crisis follows that offered by Winston Churchill in *The Gathering Storm* (New York: Bantam Books, 1961), chap. 17.

21. Ibid., p. 291.

War broke out in 1939 under less favorable conditions for the Allies than would have been the case had the leadership of Churchill and Duff Cooper prevailed in the crisis of 1938.

What about Hitler's leadership? We must admit that, given his aggressive purpose, it was brilliant—a historic bluff that worked, a desperate gamble by an evil leader that succeeded owing largely to his shrewd perception of how the constituted leaders of Britain and France were likely to respond to his threats. Had he been mistaken about this, or had Chamberlain for some reason (such as poor health) been compelled to delay his arrival in Germany for the talks that prepared the deal, the bluff might have been foiled—by a group of German military men who defined the crisis situation as such a danger to Germany that they conspired to remove Hitler and his fellow Nazi chieftains from power before he plunged the country into a great war for which, as they knew, it was not yet adequately prepared. According to a later account given by Gen. Franz Halder, who was chief of the German general staff in 1938 and who survived the war,

> By the beginning of September, we had taken the necessary steps to immunize Germany from this madman. At this time the prospect of war filled the great majority of the German people with horror. We did not intend to kill the Nazi leaders—merely to arrest them, establish a military government, and issue a proclamation to the people that we had taken this action only because we were convinced they were being led to certain disaster.[22]

It was decided, Halder went on, to strike at Hitler and other Nazi leaders at 8:00 P.M. on 14 September. But at 4:00 P.M. that day, news arrived that Chamberlain was flying to talk with Hitler at Berchtesgaden. It appeared

22. Ibid., p. 279.

that Hitler's bluff was working, and the generals abandoned their planned coup.

Churchill accepted Halder's story as genuine and cited it at length in his memoirs. Not all historians are similarly persuaded. However, the judicious and fully documented account of events by the noted German historian Karl Bracher leaves no doubt that numbers of high-placed German military men and others were conspiring to take action against Hitler in the hope of averting a war by deposing the dictator. "It was a risky, hurriedly improvised plan for a rapidly deteriorating situation," Bracher concludes. "Hitler's triumph at Munich knocked the bottom out of all these plans."[23]

After Hitler's terms were met at the Munich meeting, Chamberlain and Daladier came home to the plaudits of cheering crowds, and Chamberlain made his famous misstatement that he had brought back "peace in our time." Not long after, his conduct in the crisis had been discredited by events, and Churchill was called to leadership of a Britain that might not have been embattled had he been the constituted leader in 1938 and had his definition of the situation and proposed mode of response prevailed in Anglo-French policy. As for Hitler, his authority rose higher in Germany as a result of Munich, but the disasters and savagery that his leadership loosed upon the world made him later an object of execration among all decent people, Germans and non-Germans alike.

An inference that we might draw as students of political leadership has to do with an issue raised earlier: Shall we approach leadership as an interactional process, a relation between leaders and followers, or, alternatively, as a kind of activity that leaders seek to perform in their ca-

23. Karl Dietrich Bracher, *The German Dictatorship: The Origins, Structure, and Effects of National Socialism*, trans. Jean Steinberg (New York and Washington, D.C.: Praeger, 1970), p. 398.

pacities as leaders? Although it is possible and for some purposes necessary to view leadership in relational terms, our second example suggests that we are on stronger analytical ground when we consider leader–follower relations themselves in the context of leadership activity. For a leader's authority as a leader, his or her hold upon the followers' loyalty and willingness to follow, will depend in some measure upon the effectiveness or ineffectiveness of the leadership performance from the followers' point of view. Unless a leader who fails conspicuously in action as a leader manages to conceal the failing from the political community—as some tyrannical leaders have done, at least until their death or overthrow—that leader's authority is likely to suffer as a consequence of the perceived failure, as Chamberlain's did soon after Munich, and as Hitler's did much later. In the final analysis, the strength of leadership as an influencing relation·rests upon its effectiveness as activity.

Having set out the rudiments of a leadership approach to politics, we may now return to the question posed earlier about the alternative view that politics is the pursuit of power. If, as was argued, the power approach is critically inadequate as the basis for a general theory of politics, how can we account for its tenacious hold over time upon thoughtful minds, and the fact that no few leading political thinkers have espoused it? The nub of the answer, I believe, is that the purposes and concerns that have historically conferred meaning on circumstances in the minds of constituted political leaders have been, primarily, purposes and concerns connected with power. The situation-defining function of political leadership has been performed mainly from the angle of the question, What does the given set of circumstances confronting this political community signify for its power position in the political world, or for the power position of the ruling element or political party, or for the power position of the leader himself, or for all of these combined? Political leadership, in other words, has largely been leadership *for power*, and theorists have inferred from this fact, understandably but erroneously, that politics is in essence the pursuit of power. Erroneously, because leadership has on occasion been exercised, can be exercised, and conceivably might come in future to be exercised more and more for ends other than power.

Given the heavy accent on power in past and present political history, a political type has crystallized that is above all, as in Lasswell's formula, power-oriented. This type of human being is not the only one in the wide world of politics, but it is a commonly encountered type whose defining characteristic is effectiveness in the process of acquiring political power. We recognize the type in ordinary parlance when we say of so-and-so that he is an extremely able campaigner for office but not particularly good at governing once the sought-for political office has been won. This leader-for-power will be met with in the future, as always in the past, given the lure of power for some who are also well endowed with the skills needed to attain it. There will also, however, be political leaders for whom power is mainly an opportunity to exercise leadership for ends other than power.

But past political theorizing has understandably been responsive to past political realities, among which the power motivation of political leadership has been conspicuous. As a consequence, students of politics were led to the reductionist error of equating politics with pursuit of power. The notion of politics as a leadership process, as outlined in the foregoing pages, is more promising in the end because it is more comprehensive. It accommodates the large element of truth in the power approach by recognizing that power motivation has not

26

only been a predominant concern in past history but will also probably always be present in one degree or another in the political process. Yet, as I shall seek to show here, a leadership approach can illuminate areas of potential analysis and open up vistas for political theorizing that are not found in political study as power theorists have pursued it. The conception of politics as leadership involves the recognition that whatever material interests and power interests figure in political life—as some always do—politics is basically a realm of the mind.

Leaders and History

Whether and how leaders matter has long been a subject of controversy. Such influential writers as Marx and Tolstoy have pictured leaders (as Tolstoy portrayed Napoleon in *War and Peace*) as playthings of massive forces that move history toward unknown and predetermined ends. Others, myself included, are uncomfortable with such an outlook. We believe that not only people in the mass but also people as individuals, and particularly those who are leaders, often make a significant difference in historical outcomes by virtue of the ways in which they act or fail to act at critical junctures in the development of events. From this standpoint, history is open-ended, a fluid field of forces in which results are not rigidly predetermined even though the currents may be running strongly in one direction rather than another. The task is to specify how it is, if this is so, that leaders count in history.

The philosopher Sidney Hook addressed this question in the early 1940s in his study *The Hero in History*, which began, interestingly, by asserting "the indispensability of *leadership* in all social life, and in every major form of social organization." The problem was to determine what roles leaders play in history, and, in doing this, to steer a middle course between two mistaken extremes: on the one hand, the position of Carlyle, in *Heroes and Hero-Worship*, that "Universal History . . . is at bottom the History of the Great Men who have worked here," and, on the other hand, the position of the Spencerians, Marxists, and others who have attached little or no importance to the influence of individuals upon historical events.

Hook's solution lay in drawing a distinction between the hero as "eventful" man and the hero as "event-making" man. Both appear, he reasoned, at history's "forking-points." The former is one who happens to be present at a turning point and, by acting as he does, helps events to take the course they might in any case have been expected to take. The latter is one who causes events to take a different course from that which they would likely have taken if he had not been present. The event-making man, by virtue of "outstanding capacities of intelligence, will and character rather than of accidents of position," shapes the course of history and causes it to go *his* way. A classic exemplar was Lenin, without whose potent presence in Petrograd at the forking point of 1917 the Bolsheviks probably would not have taken power in Russia. Hook rested the case for this view partly upon the weighty testimony of Lenin's coleader in 1917, Trotsky, who, in his *History of the Russian Revolution* and again in the diary that he wrote in exile in 1935, departed from the ground of orthodox Marxism to the extent of suggesting that Lenin's leadership of the Bolsheviks was a sine qua non of their revolutionary success.

The merely eventful man was typified for Hook by Neville Chamberlain, who had supposed in his political innocence that "he could stop a war that had been in the making from the very moment Hitler assumed power." He likens the role of such merely eventful men to that of the legendary Dutch boy who saved the town by sticking his finger in the hole that he spied in the dike and holding it there until help came. It was a historic event for the town that he thereby saved. But, says Hook, "almost anybody in the situation could have done it. All that was required was a boy, a finger, and the lucky chance of passing by."[24]

With all esteem for the Dutch, young and old, I beg to differ. The action that the legendary boy took when he spied the hole in the dike and the water trickling through had to turn on his definition of the situation. The hole and the water coming through, and the resulting grave danger to the town, were objective circumstances. But their meaning depended upon the manner in which, once perceived, they related to the boy's purposes and concerns. Was it a town he would have wanted to save from harm? Then the situation was one of to-be-combated danger, and the logical response was the action that he took. But what if (we do not, I believe, know his exact age) he had been jilted by a girl who lived there? What if his main competitor in the coming ice-skating race on the canal lived there? What if a burning desire for revenge, or a compulsive need to win the race, was uppermost among his concerns? Then he might have diagnosed the situation as one of *not*-to-be-combated danger, or one of opportunity for himself, because it posed a danger to the town; and his response might have been to pass by in silence. Improbable in the extreme, knowing what we do of Dutch boys and Dutch culture. But without knowing that particular boy as an individual, no one can say: impossible.

As in this legendary case, the distinction between the

24. Sidney Hook, *The Hero in History: A Study in Limitation and Possibility* (Boston: Beacon Press, 1943), pp. 3, 14–15, 154, 171–73.

"event-making" and the "eventful" man also breaks down in the historical case of 1938. As we have indicated with the help of historical hindsight that Hook lacked when he wrote his book, Chamberlain's leadership influenced events at one of contemporary history's forking points. It helped bring on a world war that might have been averted by better, more effective leadership on behalf of the democracies. Or, it helped to bring on the war under conditions less favorable for the democracies than they would have been in 1938, when Czechoslovakia still stood as a formidable military power and Hitler's armies were not as strong as they later became. The failings of Chamberlain and Daladier as leaders resulted, in large part, from faulty diagnosis of the situation that Hitler created, and from the appeasement policy that flowed from that diagnosis. The outcome was not fatally predetermined.

For good or ill, leadership influences events. Leaders are hardly divisible into the few "event-making" ones who impose their personalities upon history and make it go their way and, on the other hand, the "eventful" ones who only help it follow the course it was going to take anyhow. The ways in which leaders count cannot accurately be expressed in such a dichotomy. They matter in degree, a little more, a little less, depending on how they diagnose those problem situations for their political communities, what responses they prescribe for meeting them, and how well they mobilize the political community's support for their decisions. The difference between the way in which one leader performs these functions and the way in which another does may not be very great. But it is not unimportant: it matters in history.

2

The Process of Political Leadership

The process of political leadership is activated, normally, when circumstances take on meaning for a political community, or some important element of it, in such a way that the existence of a political problem situation is recognized. Leadership has the threefold task of diagnosing the situation authoritatively, devising a course of action designed to resolve or alleviate the problem, and mobilizing the political community's support for the leaders' definition of the situation and their prescribed policy response. Although distinguishable for purposes of analysis, these three main functions of political leadership are not, as we shall see, separable in the minds of leaders or in political practice generally.

Signalizing

Before meaningful circumstances can be treated as a problem situation, their existence must be perceived. The facts must be known. The word *signalizing* may be used for the activity of apprising leaders of circumstances that appear meaningful enough to merit diagnosis and policy response. Signalizing is often done by the press, especially when uncensored, and by concerned citizens whose voices are reported in the press. To cite an everyday example, if a natural disaster strikes some part of a country, the reporting of it by the press, radio, and television may be instrumental in arousing leadership to define the situation as an emergency, justifying governmental assistance to the disaster-stricken area as the policy response.

A considerable part of the daily work of government consists in the gathering and processing of information for signalizing purposes. Some departments of government, the intelligence agencies, specialize in such activities. Virtually all engage in them to some extent. An agriculture ministry, for example, regularly observes and reports on the rural economy of its own and key foreign countries and signalizes to the ministry's leadership, and thence to the country's, any particularly meaningful circumstance, such as the prospect of a crop failure. The political leadership's resulting definition of the situation—as, say, the danger of widespread starvation—might bring a large-scale advance purchase of foodstuffs from abroad as the policy response.

Governmental bureaucracies do not always perform their signalizing function well and to the satisfaction of the higher political leadership. A classic reason for such failure is middle-level officialdom's desire to suppress information that would reflect poorly on its professional performance. Officials in charge of a province may, for example, suppress information on widespread distress in the province for fear that they will be held responsible and punished if the facts become known to higher leadership. The concealment of meaningful circumstances from leaders is a very old story—as old as the tale of the caliph who would roam the streets of Baghdad incognito at night to learn things about the lives of his subjects that his ministers withheld from him. A poignant Russian folk saying—"God is high and the czar is far away"—attests to the barrier that a self-protectionist officialdom constituted for simple Russians who wanted to signalize their distress to the czar. The early czars found one means of enabling their subjects literally to go over officialdom's head: a pail, into which an ordinary person could place a message, would be lowered at night on a rope from the czar's quarters in the Kremlin. How certain phenomena recur in history is shown by the fact that in mid-twentieth-century Russia a desperately distressed Soviet citizen's last resort, seldom effective, was a letter to Stalin. The frustration of signalizing may, as this suggests, derive from the leader himself. Some despotic rulers resist the receipt of "bad news" concerning conditions in need of correction. In such a case, officialdom's fear of transmitting signals of distress has a source in higher leadership itself.

Thus far the discussion has proceeded as if leadership's situation-defining activity takes place in a policy vacuum. But the real political world is not like that. In any political community at any given time, many different policies are likely to be in force based on past situation-defining and policy-devising. Programs for implementing those policies, often employing large numbers of civil servants, have been set up by government agencies with administrative responsibility in the fields concerned. Moreover, political leaders themselves may have a strong interest in the continuation of a policy whose abandonment or radical modification might reflect poorly upon their earlier wisdom and hence upon their present political strength and prospects.

Yet it often happens that new circumstances arise and take on potential meaning as a situation that calls for definition and for devising a new policy. The appropriate agencies of government will normally signalize the new circumstances to the political leaders. Thus, an intelligence agency may signalize circumstances indicating that a foreign government being supported under present policy has lost domestic support to such a degree that its long-term chances of survival are small. It may happen that such reporting is suppressed at a high level, after which it is said by disgruntled persons in the intelligence bureaucracy that "policy determines reporting rather than the other way around."

What has happened in such a case is that officials at a higher level have privately defined the reporting itself as the problem, and the suppression is their way of meeting the situation so defined. They have defined the reporting as the problem because, in their minds, the dominant concern is that the established policy of support for the foreign government in question must not be undermined. They may reason that the reporting is biased or inconclusive or that circumstances in the given foreign country will alter for the better or that increased support for that government will enable it to survive its present domestic difficulties. The signalizing efforts by their own intelligence service will thus be frustrated.

The upshot of the discussion is that the signalizing of what appear to the signalizers to be circumstances worthy of diagnosing as a problem situation and the appropriate policy response may or may not activate the process of political leadership. Whether and how it does will depend upon political leaders' interpretation of the meaning of what has been signalized to them, and that in turn will depend upon the purposes and concerns by which they themselves are guided in their leadership activity at the time, and upon the order of priority among these concerns. Thus it can happen that circumstances of dire meaning to very many people are made known to political leaders without serious political consequence because the leaders' concerns inhibit them from defining the situation as one calling for urgent action on their part.

A historic example occurred during the Second World War. Starting in 1942, the U.S. and British governments received detailed reports from occupied Europe indicating that the Nazis were proceeding methodically with the mass murder of Jews all over Europe. The Allied governments made this information public in a joint declaration of 17 December 1942 referring to reports that the German authorities were carrying out "Hitler's oft repeated intention to exterminate the Jewish people in Europe." This aroused considerable publicity and produced public pressures upon the U.S. and British governments to take steps, such as the liberalizing of immigration restrictions, to rescue as many Jews as possible from slaughter. Uppermost in the minds of the political leaders, however, were other concerns, including the concern not to divert attention and resources from the primary goal of fighting and winning the war. In their own minds, they never really defined the situation of Europe's Jews in such a way as to warrant all possible help as their policy response. What was done, chiefly the calling of an inconsequential Anglo-American conference on the matter in Bermuda in 1943 and the creation by President Roosevelt of a small War Refugee Board in January 1944, was too little and largely too late to interfere seriously with Hitler's success in effecting his genocidal "final solution."[1] Political leadership, as this episode shows, is a matter of degree. At one end of the scale it can be ineffective or no more than a semblance of leadership. That happens when leaders fail to espouse forceful policy responses to situations seen as challenges to serious political action.

The Role of Government

The role of government is not confined to the preleadership function of signaling. The agencies of gov-

1. This account is based on Arthur D. Morse, *While Six Million Died: A Chronicle of American Apathy* (New York: Random House, 1967). In *The Terrible Secret: Suppression of the Truth about Hitler's "Final Solution"* (Boston: Little, Brown, & Co., 1980), Walter Laqueur

ernment form a collective infrastructure of political leadership whose duty it is to assist the constituted leaders in performing their functions of defining situations, devising policy responses, and implementing these responses. The common practice of naming governmental agencies as departments or ministries of foreign affairs, finance, agriculture, commerce, labor, transport, and education bears witness to a common recognition in diverse political communities that there exist certain areas of special and permanent public interest in which problem situations are bound to arise from time to time and necessitate the devising of new policies that will have to be implemented by the establishment of governmental programs to monitor and administer them. Not only the signalizing of significant circumstances but also the defining of problem situations and the formulation of policy options may take place preliminarily in the governmental department concerned. In that case, the work of the higher constituted leadership is partially done for it by those who work down below.

A historically important case in point may serve as an illustration. In February 1946, George F. Kennan, then a Foreign Service officer and chargé d'affaires of the U.S. embassy in Moscow, responded to a query from the State Department for clarification on a puzzling point with what became famous as the "long telegram," an eight-thousand-word message that sought to define the problem situation being created for the United States and its Western allies by the circumstances of the Stalin government's uncooperative and expansionist conduct toward the close of the Second World War and in the war's aftermath. Not only did Kennan's telegram present a carefully reasoned diagnosis of Soviet conduct and the then emerging East–West conflict situation, but it also suggested several lines of prudent American response *in* the problem situation that it defined.[2] The "long telegram" produced an electrifying effect in and upon official Washington. It was read by the president, by members of his cabinet, and by very many U.S. government officials down the line. Essentially, this until then little known officer in the Foreign Service performed the act of political leadership that became the underpinning of America's posture in the ensuing years of the Cold War. Kennan did more than just define the problem situation persuasively and prescribe a set of rules and attitudes that should, in his view, govern U.S. policy toward Stalin's Russia. In 1947 he made an effective contribution to the mobilizing of support for the leadership's definition of the situation and proposed policy response. He did this by publishing in the journal *Foreign Affairs* an influential amplification of the "long telegram" in an article entitled "The Sources of Soviet Conduct," signed "X." Inevitably, the identity and (by now) authoritative status of Mr. X soon became public knowledge.

The adequacy of Kennan's definition of the situation is a matter for discussion in another context (as a Russianist writing from hindsight, I consider it to have been diagnostically deficient in that it located the source of the difficulties the West was encountering in the impersonal mentality of a Soviet leadership group when what should have been pinpointed was the warfare personality of the

---

suggests (pp. 203–4) that the realities were not accepted in London and Washington because "the evil nature of Nazism was beyond their comprehension," but he adds that even if the realities of the "final solution" had been accepted, "the issue would still have figured very low on the scale of Allied priorities."

2. For the text of the "long telegram" and Kennan's account of its origin, see George F. Kennan, *Memoirs 1925–1950* (Boston: Little, Brown & Co., 1967), pp. 292–95, 547–59.

autocrat Stalin). What is striking about the "long tele-gram" as a leadership act is the catalytic effect it had upon official Washington. There was a receptivity born of troubled concern over current Soviet actions in several places—Iran, the Balkans, Germany, and so forth. The Western allies were countering these actions as best they could on an ad hoc basis. Until the "long telegram" came, however, they lacked a coherent, persuasively reasoned, general definition of the situation that could underlie a coordinated set of policy responses and provide orienta-tion for action. Equipped though it was with seasoned Russian specialists, the State Department was "flounder-ing in its efforts to assess and respond to Soviet initia-tives."[3] Without the diagnosis that Kennan set forth, the American stance in the developing East–West confronta-tion was uncertain; with it, leadership was forthcoming. This is only a particular example of what the presence or absence of a persuasive definition of a situation can mean in political history.

The involvement of governments in decisions reached by individual supreme leaders may be further illustrated by reference to a well-known decision concerning which we have unusually detailed information.[4] In this instance, the meaningful circumstances were signalized to the U.S. political leadership by the Central Intelligence Agency. In October 1962 Pres. John F. Kennedy received, through photographic reconnaissance, proof that the Soviet Union was installing large numbers of offensive nuclear missiles

3. Hugh De Santis, *The Diplomacy of Silence: The American Foreign Service, the Soviet Union, and the Cold War, 1933–1947* (Chicago: University of Chicago Press, 1979), p. 175.
4. The principal source of information, and the one on which my account here is based, is Robert F. Kennedy's posthumously published book, *Thirteen Days: A Memoir of the Cuban Missile Crisis* (New York: W. W. Norton, 1969).

in Cuba, despite the fact that it had publicly and privately denied any such intention. It was estimated that within one week missiles with an atomic-warhead capacity of about half the then current Soviet ICBM potential would be operational. These missiles were targeted on U.S. cities, and it was estimated that 80 million Americans would be killed if they were fired.

The president formed an executive committee to deliberate and advise him during the few days available for secret deliberation before he would be confronted by a Soviet fait accompli. The committee's members included the vice-president, the secretaries of state and defense and their deputies, the secretary of the treasury, the attorney general (a post then held by the president's brother, Robert Kennedy), the chairman of the joint chiefs of staff, the directors of the CIA and the U.S. Information Agency, the U.S. ambassador to the United Nations, a former U.S. ambassador to Moscow, and some others, including two nonconstituted leaders, former Secretary of State Dean Acheson and former Secretary of Defense Robert Lovett, who were called in on occasion. To avoid arousing undue attention and to encourage uninhibited discussion, the president absented himself from some of the committee's sessions, which went on almost constantly during the ensuing days.

Pointing out that the overall strategic balance would remain heavily in America's favor even after installation of the new Cuba-based Soviet missiles, a small minority initially suggested that no U.S. response was necessary. But considering the adverse impact that so spectacular a Soviet move to change the balance would have on America's world political standing, the committee's majority strongly supported the president's position that inaction was out of the question (the president later agreed with his brother that inaction on his part would have led to his impeachment—thereby showing his understanding that leadership as a relation of authority is a function of leadership as effective performance). In effect, the situation was defined as a grave crisis in which some decisive action must be taken to secure the missiles' removal.

But there were differences over what the action should be. In the view of the joint chiefs of staff, with whom some civilians on the committee concurred, the United States should mount a surprise air attack with five hundred sorties against the Cuban missile sites and other military targets, such as airfields and ports. In the course of discussion, a different position was espoused by Defense Secretary Robert McNamara and Robert Kennedy. They favored a naval blockade or quarantine to stop Soviet merchant ships then on the high seas laden with missile-related equipment from reaching Cuba, and simultaneous forceful U.S. diplomatic action to compel Moscow, under threat of force, to dismantle the missiles already in place and abandon the missiles project. Although some serious arguments were raised against it, this plan won majority support in the committee. The president opted for it, and it was put into effect with success.

Seeming agreement between the two groups on the definition of the situation concealed a subtle difference. In the minds of the proponents of the air attack, a crushing military response was mandatory because of what they perceived as a Soviet motive in installing the missiles in Cuba: to demonstrate U.S. military impotence, with a view to further moves against U.S. interests elsewhere in the world, such as Berlin. The others had no clear interpretation of Soviet motives to set against this one, but they were not sure about it.[5] Here, then, as in the Munich af-

5. For John F. Kennedy's speculative view on that, see Arthur M. Schlesinger, Jr., *A Thousand Days: John F. Kennedy in the White House*

fair, in which the differing policy prescriptions of Chamberlain and Churchill turned largely on differing interpretations of Hitler's aims in creating the crisis, the diagnosis of a political situation inescapably involved an estimate of the motives of others in bringing it about.

Generalizing, it appears that when different policy responses are proposed in leadership councils, they will be correlated with differences, perhaps nuanced or even concealed, over what the situation is. Such diagnostic disagreements are likely to turn on differences over the explanation of the circumstances involved. Definitions of the situation in politics characteristically contain or imply an explanatory effort, an answer to the question, Why have these circumstances come about? In the Cuban case, as just noted, there were differing American explanations of why the missiles were being installed. Those advocating the air strike had one explanation of Moscow's motivation; those favoring the quarantine did not share that explanation, although they lacked a definite alternative one. Other examples come easily to mind. In American society today, violent urban crime is generally defined as a serious problem situation, but diagnoses of the problem differ over the causes, and these differences are correlated with different proposed remedies. Those who find the causes primarily in unemployment and related conditions that breed violent crime are apt to prescribe public policies designed to change those crime-breeding conditions, whereas people who believe that the causes lie mainly in

---

(New York: Fawcett Premier Books, 1965), p. 742. In my own view as a specialist in Soviet politics, Khrushchev undertook the Cuban missiles project as an inexpensive way to reduce U.S. superiority over the USSR in nuclear missile power without diverting to ICBM construction inside the USSR huge sums that he wanted to invest in economic development to benefit the Soviet population. Pressure on him from Soviet military groups to close the missiles gap probably was also involved.

laxity on the part of the system of criminal justice will prescribe deterrence of violent crime through a more promptly and reliably punitive system.

Governmental participation in political leadership is notable in the Cuban case. The president was assisted in his deliberation and decisionmaking by the top-level officers of the agencies of government concerned with foreign affairs. What took place during the days of crisis was a collective leadership process, about which Robert Kennedy later wrote, "And so we argued, and so we disagreed—all dedicated, intelligent men, disagreeing and fighting about the future of their country, and of mankind."[6] The collective character of the process of leadership is evident also in the way support for the decisions reached was mobilized. A legal foundation for the proposed course of action was established under the Charter of the Organization of American States, whose unanimous support for the blockade was forthcoming. Congressional leaders were briefed. Dean Acheson went as an envoy to the leader of France, President de Gaulle, who gave forceful support to the U.S. plan, as did Chancellor Adenauer of Germany. Ambassador Adlai Stevenson's persuasive presentation to the U.N. Security Council of the evidence for the Soviet deployment of the Cuban missiles and the case for the U.S. demand for their withdrawal and quarantine of the Soviet ships was a highlight of the government's effort to mobilize world support. The American ambassadors to two key African countries, Guinea and Senegal, both of which were geopolitically important in the crisis, sought and obtained their presidents' agreement and cooperation with the American plan of action.

We see in the Cuban case how the three prime lead-

6. Kennedy, *Thirteen Days*, p. 35.

ership functions are intertwined in practice. The executive committee did not try to define the situation before discussing policy responses but went directly to the latter problem, and the differing ways of defining the situation emerged in the debate over differing proposals for U.S. action. The third function of leadership—the mobilization of support—constantly preoccupied the minds of some of the principals as they considered the pros and cons of the conflicting proposals for action. In the minds of Robert Kennedy and also of the president, a decisive consideration in favor of the blockade and against the air attack was that the United States could marshal support at home and abroad for the former but not for the latter. After listening to Dean Acheson argue brilliantly that an air attack and invasion of Cuba were the only course to take, Robert Kennedy replied that whatever military reasons Acheson and others could adduce, they were advocating, in the final analysis, a surprise attack by a huge nation against a very small one, and this could not be done without destroying America's moral position at home and around the world. He recalled later that the executive committee spent more time "on this moral question" during the first five days than on any other. Thus leadership's task of mobilizing support for a policy response played a very large part in determining what that response would be. Here, then, in what might seem a case that gives weight to Lasswell's position that "the demand to coerce is the phenomenon with which we are most concerned as professional students of politics" (for this U.S.–Soviet confrontation involved, in the offing, both sides' capacity to use the supreme instrument of coercion, nuclear weapons), the crucial question was not what would be the most coercive response but what would be the most morally and politically persuasive one.

Finally, the record of American deliberation in the

missiles crisis reveals something of great importance about political problem situations, especially adversary situations: their labile character. The president had recently been reading Barbara Tuchman's *The Guns of August*, which tells how a series of moves and countermoves by the European powers led in 1914 to a world war that no one willed in advance; and he did not want some survivor of World War III to write a similar book about its origins, entitled *The Missiles of October*. So he was much preoccupied by the question of what would happen *if* the United States launched the five-hundred-sortie air raid that the joint chiefs and others were advocating. Could he be absolutely certain that *all* the already emplaced Soviet missiles would be destroyed? He was informed that he could not. Would not the air attack place insuperable pressure on the Soviet leaders to make military countermoves, if not in Cuba then elsewhere, say Berlin, and what would the United States do then? Such reasoning showed awareness that the way in which a government meets an adversary situation will modify that situation or create a new situation with its new challenge to further response, and so on—in this case possibly leading, by escalation, to a nuclear Armaggedon. Generalizing, we may say that a political adversary situation (S) is, in its development over time, a sequence of situations, such that each response (R) leads to a counterresponse (R^1) that confronts the first government with a new situation (S^1): $S—R—R^1—S^1—R—R^1—S^2—R—R^1—S^3$, and so forth.

The sequential pattern seems to be particularly characteristic of adversary situations. In many other instances, one and the same situation has a long-term character and shows development over time. Of such a situation we may say that it has a future dimension. Dynamisms present in the circumstances will cause the situation to grow more

or less serious over time, partly dependent upon what action leadership takes, or fails to take, in response. An example from contemporary American experience has to do
with the leadership of the automotive industry in the situation created by the Arab oil embargo and the resulting
gasoline shortage following the Middle Eastern war of
1973. Given those new circumstances, together with the
unsettled character of international politics, the automotive industry's leadership might have foreseen that shortages were likely to recur in the future, that fuel prices
would continually rise, and that American motorists,
however wedded by habit to large automobiles, would
eventually prefer small, economic models and switch en
masse to foreign products if the American companies did
not respond to the situation by changing their production
pattern. The failure to define the situation in terms of its
future dimension resulted, by 1980, in a financial crisis in
one of America's major industries. The example shows
that wise leadership, being (as we have always known)
foresightful, takes into account, in weighing what the response should be, the potential or probable further development of the circumstances that have already taken on
meaning as a problem situation. It assesses the situation
in its future dimension. This requires both the capacity to
analyze the causation of circumstances, and vision.

We must also consider leadership's role in relation to
situations that will predictably recur from time to time.
Legislation, and hence legislative leadership, is especially
concerned with such situations. If, for example, a legisla-
ture passes a law that attaches sanctions to a certain sort
of act, for example making terrorism a capital offense, it is
defining a predictably recurrent situation of violence or its
threat as so dangerous to the political community that enactment and application of the law in question are justified as society's policy response to future situations of that

type. Legislative leadership's purpose in such a case is to deter the commission of terrorist acts in the future. Here leadership is defining potential situations as the problem. In other words, the circumstance that has taken on meaning as a problem situation is the fact that terrorist acts have occurred and are likely to be repeated or to multiply if no preventive measures are adopted.

The challenge to forestall predictably recurrent dangerous or distressful situations, rather than simply respond to them when they occur, confronts every kind of political leadership and, indeed, leadership in all areas of society. The challenge has sometimes been met. For example, new fiscal policies adopted in the United States during the Great Depression of the early 1930s proved instrumental in forestalling the repetition of comparably grave situations of socioeconomic distress. Very often, however, leadership shows itself incapable of diagnosing potential situations as the problem and of modifying policies in such a way that those situations can be avoided in the future.

Examples are not hard to find. The chilling experience of the Cuban missiles crisis helped to generate in the leaderships of both the United States and the Soviet Union a will to cooperate, for example in arms control, in order to prevent nuclear war. Yet it remained, and remains even now, the accepted doctrine on both sides that such cooperation should and must be accompanied by a constant nonmilitary contest for political influence in third countries, Third World countries in particular. Both superpowers seek a predominant political position in the world. On neither side has leadership shown a grasp of the cooperation-destroying inner dynamics of such a "dialectical" (as it has been called in Soviet publications) combination of competition and cooperation between the two states.

Their cooperative relations are bound to suffer because, from time to time, situations will arise when one or another of the competitors finds itself about to lose influence in a particular country and is then under pressure to interpose military force in order to preserve the jeopardized position. That in turn will lead to high tension and possible military confrontation with the competing superpower, and the structure of cooperation will be badly buffeted if not destroyed. A recent case in point is Afghanistan, where Soviet military intervention in early 1980 to prevent the possible overthrow of a pro-Communist regime brought extreme tension, the shelving of an already negotiated arms-control treaty (SALT II), and virtual breakdown of U.S.–Soviet cooperation. Where or when such incidents will occur is not easily predictable, but it is predictable that they *will* occur. Yet neither of the leaderships of the superpowers has risen to the challenge of recognizing the fundamental irresponsibility of the continuing political-influence competition and of the consequent need to reexamine and modify, on both sides, the policies that recurrently darken the relations between the countries and threaten the peace of the world. The leaderships have not defined the foreseeably recurring situations of near-confrontation as a problem, and not having done that they have also not modified their policies in a way that would forestall the problem from recurring again and again in the future.

Defining Political Situations

Leaders' minds are influenced by past experience when, significant circumstances having been signalized to them, they proceed to define the current situation for the political community. Just as a person in private life has a mental repertoire of expectable situations or types of situations, so does a person in public life. Accordingly, new circumstances will be approached as potential new instances of public situations familiar from the past.

Some type-situations might be described as "archetypal" because of their immense impact upon the generation that originally experienced them and upon posterity. Robert Kennedy's account of the Cuban missiles crisis gives us a glimpse into the way in which the specter of an archetypal situation can influence the thought and conduct of a leader in power. He recalled how, as he listened to proposals for a surprise air attack on Cuba, he passed a note to his brother the president saying: "I now know how Tojo felt when he was planning Pearl Harbor." [7] He did not want his brother's government to bear the onus of responsibility for an American "day that will live in infamy."

Not only "Pearl Harbor" but also "Munich," "Depression," "Holocaust," "Hiroshima," "Cold War," and "Vietnam" have become archetypal situations in the minds of the political generations that experienced the 1930s, the Second World War, and its aftermath. It would not be surprising if the specter of "another Munich" influenced Dean Acheson when he supported the plan for a crushing military response to the Soviet missile buildup in Cuba in preference to a course of limited pressure and the use of diplomacy. Fears of a "Holocaust" situation have seemingly influenced Israeli thought and policy in confrontation with a hostile Arab world.

Those who do not remember the past are condemned to repeat it, said the philosopher George Santayana. So, we may add, are those who only remember it. Type-situations deposited by past experience can be aids

7. Ibid., p. 31.

in diagnosing new situations that arise in the present and resemble those encountered in the past in some crucial way. But if a leader's mind is fixated upon a type-situation, either negatively or positively, he may become blind to what is novel and different about a present set of circumstances, and his performance as a leader may suffer grievously as a result. A creative leader will be history-minded, but not history-obsessed. He will be mindful of Lincoln's dictum in his second inaugural address: "The dogmas of the quiet past are inadequate to the stormy present. The occasion is piled high with difficulty and we must rise to the occasion. As our case is new—so we must think anew and act anew." That expressed the philosophy of creative leadership.

We have said that political problem situations arise when circumstances take on meaning in relation to a political community's purposes and concerns. What are these? In practice, they are the community's purposes and concerns *as someone conceives them*. How any member or leader of the community conceives them will almost certainly be affected by that individual's group affiliations, his or her location in the sociopolitical world. Contemporary societies are divided along economic, sectional, ethnic, party, educational, and other lines. Very many of the groups into which they are divided are organized and have leaderships dedicated to the promotion of group interests. Characteristically, these are equated, in the minds of the group's members and leaders, with the interests—that is, the purposes and concerns—of the political community as a whole. So, a political party will regard itself as the natural custodian of those larger concerns as well as of its own. Business, labor, and other leaders will believe that the group interests to which they are responsive in their leadership roles are the interests of the nation. Those who become national political leaders will usually retain group allegiances even as they seek to be "leaders of all the people."

These considerations go a long way toward explaining the contentiousness inherent in political life, the controversies that constitute its daily stuff. Leaders of different party affiliations or from different sectors of society will predictably differ in their definitions of political situations that arise. Leaders of the party in power, seeking reelection, will find the overall state of the society good, or at any rate far better than when the party took office, whereas leaders of the party that seeks to oust them will find the society in a serious problem situation caused by policies of the present leadership and will proclaim the need for a new set of policies aimed at rectifying this unfortunate state of affairs.

How leaders' responsiveness to different concerns underlies differences in their ways of defining the political community's situation may be illustrated by a discussion that took place in the United States in 1975. At that time the leader of organized labor, George Meany, proposed to define the then prevailing 8 percent–plus level of unemployment as a "depression," whereas those in the government, headed by Secretary of the Treasury William Simon, wanted to define it as a "recession." Mr. Meany was evoking an archetypal situation as a means of promoting labor's special interest in full employment. If the problem situation were to be defined as a "depression," there would be more congressional and public support for policies aimed at alleviating unemployment rapidly and drastically. No doubt the labor leadership believed that such remedial measures would be in the country's interest as well as labor's. The official definition of the situation as a "recession," on the other hand, implied need for less far-reaching remedial measures and, in addition, served the party interest of an administration that would soon be campaigning for reelection. Given the archetype "Depression" in the public mind, it would be politically harmful for a party in power to be seen as the custodian of an economy gone into a depression.

This example may raise in the reader's mind the question, Which comes first, the definition of the situation (as here argued) or the policy prescription? We must allow that a leader's policy preferences, deriving perhaps from professional specialization or group allegiance, can influence that leader's mode or tendency of situation-defining. Thus a professional labor mediator may be inclined by experience and training to define situations of management–labor conflict in ways that make them appear amenable to successful mediation. That is not, however, to say that policy prescriptions underly definitions of the situation. In the case just discussed, Mr. Meany would not have proposed remedial measures at all if the rate of unemployment in the country had been so low that he did not diagnose a problem situation. On the other hand, once he had so diagnosed it, his *public* definition of the situation as a "depression" can be seen as a means of being persuasive in his advocacy of more far-reaching remedial steps than others wanted to take. In short, once a situation has been defined in his or her mind, a leader may accentuate its seriousness in public statements so as to make the resulting policy proposals more persuasive. This simply reflects a fact already noted, that public definitions of the situation in politics perform a mobilizing function along with the diagnostic one.

Sectional interests also come into play in leadership's performance of the diagnostic function. Thus in 1979 an ocean oil-well blowout occurred in the Gulf of Mexico. The resulting spill remained out of control for a long while. Escaping oil coated beaches along the Texas Gulf

Coast, threatening onshore and offshore ecosystems and adversely affecting commercial fisheries. Inevitably, the circumstances, although they took on meaning for the entire U.S. political community, especially impinged upon the purposes and concerns of people in the affected area and took on particularly poignant meaning for them and leaders representing them. On the other hand, since the blowout occurred in an oil well being drilled by the Mexican government, and since the U.S. Department of State was then engaged in negotiations with the Mexican government over oil and gas sales to the United States, the department reportedly "muffled all national concern over the spill."[8] Given the concerns by which the State Department was guided in its negotiations with Mexico, the harmful effects of the Mexican spill did not seem sufficiently meaningful to justify a definition of the Gulf Coast situation in such serious terms as seemed right to local residents.

When compounded by ethnic, racial, or religious cleavages, sectional differences can reach such a pitch of acuteness that leaders' definitions of the situation go beyond the bounds of rational discussion and debate. A movement for self-determination may emerge within a disadvantaged part of a nation-state, for example, and the movement's leadership may define the situation as a "struggle for national liberation." The nation-state's governmental leadership will doubtless define it as "sedition" or a "secessionist struggle." As a result, armed action seems the only possible policy response on both sides. Recent world political history offers numerous examples.

Here (and not for the last time on these pages) the question of the validity of definitions of the situation

8. Eric Schneider, "The Mexican Oil Gushes On and On," *The New York Times*, 26 February 1980.

arises. In this hypothetical case, is each of the clashing definitions of the situation valid in relation to the given group's purposes and concerns? Do we have, as in Marx's discussion in *Capital* of the struggle over the length of the working day, "an antinomy, right against right," of which we have to say with Marx, "Between equal rights, force alone decides"?[9] So a power theorist of politics might see it. From a leadership standpoint, however, a different approach seems possible. The validity of definitions of the situation may be a matter of degree. There is a possibility, theoretical if not practical in any particular case, of a more inclusive diagnosis that would make room for some, if not all, of the purposes and concerns on both sides. Conciliatory leadership, thinking in humane terms, might define the situation neither as a struggle for national liberation nor as sedition, but as a combination of injustices toward the population of the rebellious area and self-perpetuating misery-producing conflict growing out of those injustices. Such a definition of the situation might logically lead to outside mediation of the conflict as the policy response. The aim that leadership would hope to fulfill through mediation would be a settlement that would take into account, so far as possible, the vital concerns of both groups.

Along with such cleavages of interest as those already discussed, an analyst of politics must consider those that arise within governments. The collective infrastructures of leadership, like the societies over which they preside, are not always like-minded in performing their pre-leadership functions. Such like-mindedness may in fact be more the exception than the rule, and this seems as true of authoritarian one-party states as of constitutional

9. *The Marx-Engels Reader*, ed. Robert C. Tucker, 2d ed. (New York: W. W. Norton, 1978), p. 364.

democracies. Leaders of different departments of one and the same government often differ in their proposed definitions of the situation and in their prescriptions for policy because circumstances will have different meanings for agencies with different missions, depending on the particular purposes or concerns of the political community that they exist to serve.

Thus, the defense department of a government, charged with the military concern, may minimize the danger to arms-control efforts inherent in a proposed new weapons system that is designed to enhance the nation's warmaking power, whereas the government's arms-control agency (if it has one), being the steward of a different national purpose, may assess as very high the danger that development of that weapons system represents to future achievement in arms-control policy. Or, to cite a concrete case from recent American experience, it was reported in 1979 that the Department of State and Department of Justice were at odds over possible admission of large numbers of persons fleeing Vietnam in boats. The State Department, concerned with America's prestige abroad, defined the problem situation created by the "boat people" as sufficiently serious to justify immediate admission of twenty-five thousand of them, whereas Justice, whose prime concern lay in following usual immigration procedures, was not inclined to accept so serious a definition of the situation and so dramatic a departure in immigration policy.[10]

When such divisions occur, higher leadership must choose. The choice often turns on more than just an intellectual analysis of the "trade-offs" involved in choosing one concern over another, or the perception of how one or another way of deciding the question will serve, say, the

10. *The New York Times*, 2 March 1979.

leader's concern for the strengthening of his own or his party's power. It will involve, as well, those aspects of personality that can be summed up under the heading of "values and feelings," including compassion, or the lack of it, for the people who will be affected by the final decision. A Lasswellian *homo politicus*, preoccupied exclusively with accentuating his power, will be sensitive only to those concerns of others that may prove beneficial or detrimental to his power position. Alternatively, sensitivity can mean the vicarious sharing of others' concerns, the capacity to feel them.

For example, at the outset of the 1960s both the United States and the Soviet Union were still testing nuclear weapons aboveground. Huge quantities of radioactive fallout were released into the atmosphere, then came down onto grass that was eaten by cows that produced milk that people, babies included, drank. Scientists studied these circumstances and their harmful effects on animals and people. One day President Kennedy's science adviser, Jerome Wiesner of MIT, brought scientists into the White House to explain these circumstances to the president. But it was up to him to define the problem situation, which turned on the relative importance of the health hazard to people compared with what it would mean to U.S. defense preparedness if the then intensive program of atmospheric nuclear testing was discontinued; and probably the definition of the situation in some quarters of the government stressed the latter concern. According to an account of the meeting with the scientists, "It was a rainy day, and the President asked whether radioactivity was right there—in the rain. Yes, he was told, it was. He stood silent for minutes, looking out of the window of the White House at the rain."[11] His

11. Anthony Lewis, "Memory and Desire," *The New York Times*, 22 October 1979.

feelings and values must have led him to define the atmospheric-testing situation as too dangerous to be permitted to continue for long. The outcome was a policy of negotiating an agreement with the Soviet Union under which both nations ceased aboveground nuclear tests.

Feelings that influence leaders' ways of defining political situations may relate to the leaders themselves. In a pathbreaking early study, Lasswell hypothesized that those who become active in political life characteristically displace "private affects" or motives, in other words, feelings directed toward family members or themselves, onto "public objects," such as officials or symbols of authority, that they rationalize this displacement in terms of public interests and, having done so, lose consciousness of the self- or family-referential nature of the feelings that actuate them. Thus, Lasswell suggested, a regicide may be driven by unconscious hatred of his own father that has been displaced onto a public object, the king.[12]

This hypothesis is open to serious question when treated as a universal formula. In all probability, it is more applicable to some people in political life than to others, and in any given leader's case more applicable on some occasions than on others. The important truth to which it points, however, is that the public world of the leader-as-political-actor is not insulated from the private world of the leader-as-person. In all sorts of ways, feelings and fantasies that motivate leaders' lives as individuals may intrude upon their performances in leadership roles. It is not hard to conceive, for example, that a glory-bent leader of proved or merely imagined prowess in war might consciously or unconsciously maneuver political events toward military showdowns with adversary states.

Psychological biography of political leaders, al-

12. Harold D. Lasswell, *Psychopathology and Politics*, rev. ed. (New York: The Viking Press, 1960), pp. 74–76.

though still in its formative stages as a form of scholarship, can already begin to support this argument with instances from political history. It appears that a driving need to play the hero in public life and gain vindication impelled Woodrow Wilson to take steps in his leadership roles that aroused powerful opposition, notably Dean West's to the graduate-college project that Wilson espoused as president of Princeton and Senator Lodge's to ratification of the Treaty of Versailles when Wilson was president of the United States; and then he would define the public situation as one of confrontation between right and wrong, with himself in the role of heroic defender of the right.[13] The self-dramatizing Joseph Stalin fashioned a revolutionary hero-script for himself. Aspiring to outdo his predecessor, Lenin, in exploits of revolutionary leadership, he defined Soviet Russia's internal situation in the later 1920s as analogous to that in Russia on the eve of the October Revolution of 1917.[14] His policy response was a revolution from above in the countryside, accomplished by terrorizing the peasants into joining collective farms to which most were opposed.

In both cases the outcomes were tragic. Instead of scoring the sought-for vindicatory triumphs, Wilson went down to searing defeats, with failure to bring America into the League of Nations a cost of his conflict with Lodge. Stalin's attempt to bring off a rural revolution surpassing Lenin's October Revolution in historical significance produced the worst famine in Russia's history, with

13. This interpretive comment on Wilson is based on material in Alexander and Juliette George, *Woodrow Wilson and Colonel House: A Personality Study* (New York: Dover, 1964), and draws upon Robert C. Tucker, "The Georges' Wilson Reexamined: An Essay on Psychobiography," *The American Political Science Review* 71: 2 (June 1977): esp. p. 618.

14. Robert C. Tucker, *Stalin as Revolutionary: A Study in History and Personality* (New York: W. W. Norton, 1973).

a toll of many millions of peasant lives. These and other cases in which political leaders have engineered and defined political situations according to the dictates of neurotic ego-needs raise an important question for future research: how can societies learn to develop and choose psychologically self-aware human beings for roles of leadership? By diagnosing neurotically motivated leadership activity as a problem for investigation, political science can possibly take a part in leadership itself.

Whether it is a pathology of the leadership process that we are studying or the process in its more normal manifestations, our chief laboratory for research is political history. What it means to study political history from a leadership standpoint is indicated by the foregoing discussion. In approaching any historical episode of leadership or attempted leadership, the student of politics must focus attention on who the leaders were and how they performed the functions of defining a problem situation for the political community, devising a policy response, and mobilizing support for the one and the other. He must investigate how the action subsequently taken by the government gave effect to these activities of leadership, insofar as it did, and with what consequences for the leaders and the political community.

Much of this was said long ago by the historian and philosopher of history R. G. Collingwood, who contended that the writing of history involves the reenacting of the thought of those whose purposive action is the subject of historical inquiry. Suppose, he said, the historian is studying the Theodosian Code and wants to explain an edict of an emperor:

> In order to do that he must envisage the situation with which the emperor was trying to deal, and he must envisage it as that emperor envisaged it. Then he must see for himself, just as if that emperor's situation were his own,

how such a situation might be dealt with; he must see the possible alternatives, and the reasons for choosing one rather than another; and thus he must go through the process which the emperor went through in deciding this particular course.[15]

Expressing it in our slightly different terms, the historian studying a leader's purposive political action must reenact that leader's definition of the political situation. In doing so, he will naturally make use, as evidence, of whatever that leader is known to have said, in public or in private, with respect to the situation, of what others may have said who were in positions of trust or influence, of later testimony by the leader or other informed persons, and, not least, of the action that flowed from and gave effect to the leader's way of defining the situation. To this we may add a point that Collingwood missed: psychobiographical understanding of a leader can be essential to the success of the political historian's project of reenacting past thought.

Mobilizing Support

The political process is influenced by many a material factor, but it has its prime locus in the mind. Not only is it a mental process when leaders learn about and analyze the causes of circumstances that have arisen, when they interpret the circumstances' meaning in relation to various concerns, when they define the problem situation for their political communities and decide on what seems the proper prescription for collective action. Mental processes are also pivotally involved—now in the minds of followers or potential followers—when leadership appeals for positive response to its policy prescription.

15. R. G. Collingwood, *The Idea of History* (Oxford: Oxford University Press, 1956), p. 283. See also the discussion of Caesar on p. 215.

Paraphrasing and at the same time radically revising the dictum of Harold Lasswell cited above, the need to *persuade* is the phenomenon with which we are most concerned as professional students of politics. The necessity for leadership to be persuasive arises within the precincts of government itself. The political scientist Richard Neustadt quotes President Truman as saying, when he was in the White House, "I sit here all day trying to persuade people to do the things they ought to have sense enough to do without my persuading them. . . . That's all the powers of the President amount to." Neustadt goes on: "Here is testimony that despite his status he does not get action without argument. Presidential power is the power to persuade."[16] This judgment might be still more applicable to constitutional democracies with systems of cabinet government that lack a chief executive with the prerogatives of an American president.

Once a government has been persuaded, it becomes necessary for leadership to persuade the populace. It may proceed indirectly by persuading the legislative assembly to pass a law embodying the new policy. The law, in turn, may be obeyed largely because of fear of sanctions attendant upon its violation. But widespread evasion of unpopular laws attests to the great difficulty of implementing a policy when people in large numbers remain unpersuaded of its desirability. Moreover, very many policies fall short of being legally binding. Leadership's task is to sway people's minds toward acceptance of them in practice. All sorts of manipulative techniques may come into play at this stage, but reasoned argument also has a place in the process. Not for nothing have eloquence and rhetorical ability been associated since ancient times with

16. Richard E. Neustadt, *Presidential Power: The Politics of Leadership* (New York: John Wiley, 1960), pp. 9–10.

effective political leadership. In some cases, of course, the qualities that make for effectiveness in the mobilizing of support are not combined in one and the same person with those that are requisite for the situation-defining and policy-devising tasks.

It is tempting to characterize democratic government as government by persuasion, because constitutional democracies are so organized that the executive leadership, even apart from the periodic need to face the people in an election, must persuade popularly elected legislatures before measures are adopted that have the force of law. But the need to persuade and the practice of persuasion are not something unique to democratic governments and alien to authoritarian political systems. True, there are terroristic despotisms in which a ruler manages, by the wide and arbitrary use of coercion in frightful forms, to so paralyze people with fear, from ministers in the regime to citizens in the street, that he is virtually freed from the need to persuade; the terror-tinged atmosphere of life ensures compliance. But most authoritarian governments, most of the time, are not terroristic despotisms. In many, leadership is exercised by an oligarchy within which the principal leader does not dictate his will but rather seeks to persuade fellow oligarchs of the validity of his diagnoses and plans of action.

Although the essence of authoritarianism is the arbitrary power to coerce, authoritarian regimes characteristically strive to mobilize popular support for their policies by persuasion before resorting to the coercive methods that they hold in reserve for use when persuasion fails. Two considerations cast light on why this is so. First, coercion can produce passive compliance with orders, but generally no more than that. Only if people are really persuaded of the correctness of a policy will they, as a rule, give it their active support—and authoritarian regimes very much want active support in order to ensure the successful functioning of their societies and polities. Second, authoritarian regimes are faced with a problem in the mobilizing of support that democracies generally avoid by virtue of the persuading of legislatures that often precedes and preconditions the enactment of a new policy. Insofar as the democracies' legislatures reflect public opinion, the policies they enact will have undergone some meaningful advance test of their acceptability to the public in the process of being enacted. Authoritarian regimes, on the other hand, do not have to contend with public opinion in the course of the policymaking process and, as a result, are all the more dependent upon ex post facto persuasive efforts once policies are promulgated. They may make a show of persuading the public in advance by, for example, staging a discussion of a proposed new law in the controlled official press (with approving letters outnumbering disapproving ones twenty to one) and by making their regime-controlled legislatures simulate the behavior of democratic ones in enacting new laws. But few citizens are fooled by these devices.

Whatever the system of government, people do not normally give their active support to a policy unless they are persuaded, unless leadership has cogently communicated to them its view of the nature of the problem situation to which the policy is offered as a desirable response. An example from contemporary American experience is the reluctance of many citizens to heed calls for gasoline conservation because, in part, of the difficulty the government has encountered in convincing them that the energy problem is real. The importance of a persuasive definition of the situation in the mobilizing of support for a policy may, further, be illustrated by an example, so to speak, in reverse.

A popular uprising occurred in Communist-ruled

Hungary in 1956. At that time the Hungarian leader was a liberal Communist, Imre Nagy. On 4 November 1956, the Soviet Union began a massive armed invasion of Hungary to put down the rebellion. The chairman of Hungary's Revolutionary Council of National Defense, Bela Kiraly, later a resident of New Jersey and the source of this account, could do nothing because his troops had orders not to fire on Soviet troops save in an ultimate emergency. He realized, as he later expressed it, that "the defenders needed a specific, dramatic command that it was all-out war and to act accordingly." Without, in other words, an authoritative public definition of the situation as a state of war and a command to resist the Soviet army, the Hungarian soldiers could not be expected to rise in defense of their invaded land. Kiraly phoned Nagy and advised him that the only way to make the troops aware of the real situation was for either Nagy or Kiraly to announce over Radio Budapest that Hungary was at war with the USSR. Nagy refused.[17] Since he was later executed by the Soviet authorities on charges of treason to the Communist cause, it is not credible that he refused because of being a secret collaborator of the Kremlin. In all probability, he refused because he privately diagnosed the situation as hopeless and knew that if he or Kiraly publicly defined it as a state of war and commanded the troops to fight, they would do so with wholesale and ultimately useless loss of life; it was not his intention that this should happen. The policy that followed from his private definition of the situation was inaction in response to Kiraly's plea. Here, then, the potentially mobilizing effect of a public definition of a situation is shown by the literally demobilizing effect of a public nondefinition of one.

17. Bela K. Kiraly, "Budapest, Twenty Years Ago," *The New York Times*, 23 October 1976.

Considering the persuasive power of dramatic public definitions of a political community's situation, it is not surprising that some political leaders have resorted to the expedient of contriving circumstances that enabled them to define a situation in a way that justified actions they wished to take. For example, soon after Hitler became chancellor of Germany under the Weimar Constitution in January 1933, a fire broke out in the building that housed the German parliament, the Reichstag, in Berlin. Although the cause is still in dispute among historians, the weight of the evidence supports the view that the Nazis themselves contrived to set the Reichstag afire. But they proclaimed the Communists guilty of the crime and defined the situation as a Communist plot against the state. On this basis they put through the Enabling Act that gave Hitler dictatorial powers.

Hitler's example was not lost on his Moscow contemporary, Stalin, who in 1934 secretly organized the assassination of the Leningrad party leader, Sergei Kirov. Having contrived this crime, he used it to dramatize a public definition of the situation as an anti-Communist plot against the Soviet state and proceeded on this basis to conduct a terroristic purge that made him into the dictator he was by the later 1930s; the Kirov murder was Stalin's Reichstag fire. To take a further example, in Greece in 1967 a group of colonels carried out a coup d'etat against the democratic government and set up a dictatorship after declaring the nation in danger from a Communist conspiracy. Prior to their action and this public definition of the situation that was used to elicit support for it, various circumstances were contrived. Hammer-and-sickle symbols appeared in the provinces, and fires were lit in the streets of Athens. These circumstances were reportedly contrived by persons in the security forces who favored the success of the colonels' plot to seize dictatorial power.

Such incidents might seem to contravene our thesis that leaders' definitions of a situation precede and underlie their prescriptions for political action. For here certain policy intentions, such as the Enabling Act in Hitler's case, preceded and inspired the definition of the situation as a state of emergency caused by a Communist plot. In fact, we must presume that in every case the leader or leaders had privately defined the national situation as being ripe for the assumption of dictatorial powers, and that the contriving of circumstances to support a false picture of the situation was the action taken. In these episodes, then, the official public definition of the situation is to be seen as an element of the policy response. Thus Hitler must have privately defined the situation as an opportunity to become fully the Führer now that he was chancellor. Contriving the Reichstag fire and publicly defining Germany's situation as an emergency was his way of solving the problem.

In these incidents, circumstances were contrived by persons in political authority, hence "from above." Contrivance, but "from below," takes place in the widespread present-day phenomenon of revolutionary terrorism. This takes the form of violent political actions, such as assassinations of public figures, political kidnappings, seizures of public buildings, hostage-taking, and the like. By contriving, in other words, perpetrating, these well-publicized acts of violence, terrorists aim to dramatize their public definition of the political situation and thereby to mobilize popular support for their cause. Alternatively, their terrorist acts are designed to provoke the constituted political authorities into violent reprisals that will, it is calculated, help produce fully revolutionary situations, in other words, conditions that people whose support they wish to mobilize will experience as so oppressive that they will heed the terrorists' call for revolutionary mass action.

A Brazilian manual for terrorists that has been described as an international bible for revolutionary terrorists explains the latter tactic as follows:

> The rebellion of the urban guerrilla and his persistence in intervening in public questions is the best way of insuring public support of the cause we defend. . . The government has no alternative except to intensify repression. The police networks, house searches, arrests of innocent people and of suspects, closing of streets, make life in the city unbearable. . . The political situation in the country is transformed into a military situation in which the gorillas appear more and more to be the ones responsible for errors and violence, while the problems in the lives of the people become truly catastrophic.[18]

A still more complex case was the Iranian seizure and holding of American diplomatic hostages in 1979–1980. Here action was taken both from above and from below. The authorities themselves adopted the tactics of revolutionary terrorism by contriving circumstances—the holding of the hostages—designed to dramatize their definition of a situation of hostile confrontation between revolutionary Iran and the United States, and to evoke U.S. countermeasures that would help them persuade their populace that Iran was embattled and thus to mobilize continued mass support for their cause.

It is not always necessary to contrive circumstances in order to fabricate a definition of a situation. Simple

18. Carlos Marighella, "Minimanual of the Urban Guerrilla," published as an appendix in Robert Moss, *Urban Guerrilla Warfare*, Adelphi Papers, No. 79 (London: The International Institute for Strategic Studies, 1971), p. 40.

falsification of circumstances may suffice. A historic case in point occurred in Germany in August 1914, when the kaiser's government initiated hostilities by ordering the German army to invade neutral Belgium and Luxembourg. The German people were deliberately misinformed about these circumstances. The government put out the false news that Russian forces had crossed the German border on 1 August and that French airmen had bombed Karlsruhe and Nuremberg. As a result, according to historian Julius Braunthal, the Germans "believed that they had been attacked by the Russians and the French and that their country was threatened with invasion."[19] So, they marched off to the Great War under the wrong impression that they were defending a Fatherland that was under enemy attack. We could hardly find a better illustration of the Thomas theorem, "If men define those situations as real, they are real in their consequences."

Leadership and Democracy

Most students of politics recognize the importance of the distinction between democracy and authoritarianism, and a theoretical view of politics ought to cast some light upon the reasons for its importance. What has the leadership perspective to contribute?

First, it suggests that we might fruitfully approach the distinction in terms of leadership's situation-defining and policy-devising functions. The implication is that democracy and authoritarianism can be matters of degree in the workings of a government. We are led to focus attention on the question of how the leadership process is

19. Julius Braunthal, *History of the International*, Vol. 2: 1914–1943 (New York: Frederick A. Praeger, 1967), pp. 10–11.

organized within a regime. How collegial is its decision-making and decision-discussing process? Is the principal leader relatively open-minded or relatively closed-minded? Does he or she invite high-level associates in government to state and forcefully defend their proposed definitions of the problem situation at hand and their prescriptions for policy? The answers to questions like these will help clarify highly significant differences of degree.

By approaching the problem in these terms, moreover, we can see the possibility of an authoritarian personality serving as leader in the regime of a constitutional democracy, and, conversely, of a democratic personality serving as the leader in an authoritarian system of rule. We can see, for example, how important a difference it made in Soviet politics whether the leader was the tyrannical Stalin or the domineering yet relatively open-minded Khrushchev, even though there were few outward changes in the structure of the Soviet polity between Stalin's time and Khrushchev's.

Yet the institutional difference between democratic and authoritarian forms of government (taking into account that both forms come in a multitude of varieties) should not be minimized. From the leadership perspective, democratic government entails primarily the institutionalized possibility of active public participation in the defining of problem situations for the political community. This, in turn, goes directly to the matter of freedom of assembly and all other forms of freedom of expression, above all the rights of free speech and press. The point is that without freedom of speech, press, and assembly, ordinary citizens in a political community cannot reliably and effectively participate in the preleadership function of signalizing the existence of circumstances that take on meaning as problem situations because of the way they impinge upon the citizens' purposes and concerns. Only rarely, as in the outbreak of war, do circumstances immediately take on import for the entire political community. In the usual course of things circumstances have differential impact, affecting initially and particularly the people of some locality, occupation, industry, economic level, age group, ethnic group, or so forth. Only when citizens are secure in the rights of free speech and assembly, the right to strike, and so on, can they act without hindrance to bring the circumstances and their concern over them to the attention of the general public and the authorities and to seek recognition of their own problem situation as the political community's.

Freedom of press and of publishing, and freedom of research through untrammeled access to sources of information, are vital requisites of democratic leadership. The press, which has been called the "fourth branch of government," can only function as that when it functions autonomously and apart from government. This proposition can best be argued from the negative standpoint by noting the normal abridgement of freedom of expression by authoritarian governments. Such governments may, as in Soviet Russia, encourage the controlled press to signalize circumstances whose existence runs counter to governmental policy, for example the failure of local authorities to comply with one or another party directive. But if, for any reason, the circumstances, however meaningful, are consistent with governmental policy, or if publicity about them would be contrary to the authorities' interests or wishes, censorship and other forms of control may prevent public signalizing and open diagnosis of a political situation. Since, as a result, the public is not aware of the circumstances' existence, the government is under far less pressure than would otherwise be the case to define them as a problem and to draw the necessary conclusions for present and future policy.

To cite an example, a nuclear disaster occurred in late 1957 or early 1958 in the south Ural Mountains region in the eastern USSR. It appears to have been caused by an explosion of nuclear waste material stored underground. Radioactive materials were scattered by the wind over an area of as much as a thousand square miles, forcing evacuation of towns and villages and causing an unknown number of deaths from radiation poisoning. But the disaster was never reported in the state-controlled Soviet press. It was first revealed in 1976 by an expatriate Soviet scientist, Zhores Medvedev, then living in London.[20] State control of the communications media prevented the explosion from ever entering into the public political process of the USSR. A little reflection on the more recent and apparently less injurious accident at Three Mile Island in Pennsylvania highlights the role that freedom of public expression plays in activating the leadership process.

Another case in point has to do with polio in Brazil. Some years ago, Dr. Albert B. Sabin, the American discoverer of an oral antipolio vaccine, organized an immunization campaign that proved effective in ending the spread of polio in the south Brazilian state of Santa Catarina. Later, the Brazilian health authorities informed the World Health Organization that the incidence of polio in Brazil had declined by 86 percent. But when Dr. Sabin was summoned to Brazil in 1980 to deal with a fresh outbreak of the disease, he found evidence that the information given to the World Health Organization was false. His attempt to signalize the alarming circumstances in a letter to the president of Brazil proved ineffectual. It led to

20. "The Lesson of the Poisoned Urals," *The New York Times*, 7 March 1980. For a full account, see Zhores A. Medvedev, *Nuclear Disaster in the Urals* (New York: W. W. Norton, 1979).

his dismissal as a consultant to the Brazilian government. The resulting setback to the political leadership process is shown by something said in Sabin's letter, made public in the United States: "Brazil needs a national program of vaccination against polio, organized in a highly efficient form and conducted annually." A Brazilian journalist commented (orally), "Our problem isn't infantile paralysis but adult paralysis."[21]

From the leadership perspective on politics, a key criterion for evaluating political systems along the spectrum from democracy to authoritarianism is the relative scope of opportunity that a society affords for the activities of what I have called "nonconstituted" leaders. This can best be shown by examples. A woman named Rachel Carson, who had a love of wildlife, much technical knowledge, and writing talent, published a book in 1962 called *Silent Spring*. The idea for the title came to her from a line by Keats about winter, when "The sedge is wither'd from the lake and no birds sing." Given her concerns as a lover of wildlife, especially of birds, certain circumstances took on ominous meaning in her mind. Between the 1940s and 1960s, she wrote, over two hundred basic chemicals were created in American laboratories for killing insects, weeds, rodents, and other so-called pests; they were (and are) called *pesticides* and applied in sprays, dusts, and aerosols to farms, gardens, forests, and homes. Her book's title conjured up the haunting image that conveyed her definition of the situation: a spring would come when no birds would sing. She wrote, "The pollution of our world is happening," and said that this pointed ultimately to "the pollution of the total environment of mankind." The policy prescription flowing from

21. Warren Hoge, "Brazil Slams the Door on Sabin over Polio Disclosure," *The New York Times*, 17 April 1980.

her definition of the situation was: Strictly control and drastically reduce, if not eliminate, the use of chemical pesticides.

She knew that her definition of the problem and proposed response were controversial. The prevailing practice in our society at that time was nondefinition of the danger situation, largely because of ignorance of the facts in the public mind. Behind the nondefinition of the situation, powerful influences were at work. As she put it, "The control men in state and federal governments—and of course the chemical manufacturers—steadfastly deny the facts reported by the biologists and declare they see little evidence of harm to wildlife. Like the priest and the Levite in the biblical story, they choose to pass by on the other side and to see nothing."[22] So, Carson became a nonconstituted leader, a foremost figure in the environmental movement that grew up in America, partly in response to *Silent Spring*. A U.S. secretary of the interior, Stewart Udall, recognized her importance as a leader when he said of her, "A great woman has awakened the nation by her forceful account of the dangers around us. We owe much to Rachel Carson."

Lest this account convey the impression that all nonconstituted leaders are admirable, a case of different character merits mention. Like Rachel Carson, the British psychologist Cyril Burt had some deep-seated beliefs and values. He believed in the rightness and inevitability of a class system of society. In his long, distinguished career, during which he held the influential post of editor of the *British Journal of Statistical Psychology*, he published numerous research findings supporting the view that people in the upper class were hereditarily superior in intelligence. His reported findings were that separated

22. Rachel Carson, *Silent Spring* (New York: Fawcett, 1962), p. 84.

identical twins, brought up in different environments, remained alike in I.Q. His definition of human intelligence as hereditarily determined underlay a prescription for educational policy that children, after being tested at age eleven, be separated into three groups: only those with higher intelligence should be trained in elite schools preparatory for higher education, and the (working-class) majority would be schooled as befitted their lower genetic potentials. This was adopted as British educational policy after the Second World War, and Burt was rewarded with a knighthood for his services to education. His claimed research findings concerning separated identical twins were, however, subsequently exposed as thoroughly fraudulent.[23] He had derived his policy prescription from a diagnosis of human intelligence founded on fabricated circumstances. Although an effective nonconstituted leader, considering the impact of his work on educational policy, he was not an admirable one.

Nonconstituted leaders flourish best in conditions of political freedom that afford them full opportunity to put forward their definitions of the situation and their policy prescriptions in public and to seek to mobilize followings. In authoritarian political settings, where citizens lack free access to the media of public communication, nonconstituted leadership faces great obstacles and has correspondingly limited prospects of success. Nevertheless, no few unusual individuals have surmounted all the obstacles. A well-known contemporary example is the Russian nuclear physicist, Academician Andrei Sakharov.

Having led the project to create a Soviet hydrogen bomb, Sakharov in the 1950s was a much-decorated fore-

23. Leon J. Kamin, *The Science and Politics of I.Q.* (New York: Halsted Press, 1974), and L. S. Hearnshaw, *Cyril Burt Psychologist* (Ithaca, N.Y.: Cornell University Press, 1980).

most figure in the scientific establishment, so highly valued that a special railway car, reportedly, would be placed at his disposal when he needed to travel. He began his political activity by working within the system. In 1958 he sought out Khrushchev for an interview in which he unsuccessfully tried to persuade the premier to cancel a scheduled nuclear test. In memoirs dictated long afterward, in retirement, Khrushchev recalled:

> He was obviously guided by moral and humanistic considerations. . . . He was, as they say, a crystal of morality among our scientists. . . . He was devoted to the idea that science should bring peace and prosperity to the world, that it should help preserve and improve the conditions for human life. He hated the thought that science might be used to destroy life, to contaminate the atmosphere, to kill people slowly by radioactive poisoning. However, he went too far in thinking he had the right to decide whether the bomb he had developed could ever be used in the future.[24]

Later, Sakharov was instrumental in getting the Soviet government to agree to conclude the 1963 treaty with the Americans banning further aboveground nuclear tests by the two nations.

His decisive move toward becoming a nonconstituted leader was the writing of a memorandum, "Progress, Coexistence, and Intellectual Freedom," which circulated in typescript and made its way West, where its publication in 1968 brought world fame to the author. Although he lost his favored position, he went on speaking his mind to fellow Soviet citizens and foreign correspondents. Gradually he grew convinced that the key

24. *Khrushchev Remembers: The Last Testament*, trans. and ed. Strobe Talbott (New York: Little, Brown, 1974), p. 69. For Sakharov's path to dissent, see the autobiographical introduction to *Sakharov Speaks*, ed. Harrison E. Salisbury (New York: Vintage Books, 1974), pp. 29–54.

problem was the denial of human rights in the closed Soviet society, and he became an outstanding leader of the unofficial human-rights movement in the USSR. In an essay entitled "Alarm and Hope," written in 1977 for the Norwegian Nobel Committee, at its request, he wrote: "A deeply cynical caste society has come into being, one which I consider dangerous (to itself as well as to all mankind). . . . It is precisely the society's 'closed' nature which facilitates the nation's expansionist capabilities and simultaneously secures its anti-democratic stability despite failures, by Western standards, in satisfying social needs."[25] His outspoken condemnation of the Soviet military occupation of Afghanistan in 1980 was followed by his exile to house arrest in Gorky. A mighty government exposed its inner weakness by silencing the one leader of great moral stature produced by Russia in the later twentieth century.

There are many would-be nonconstituted leaders for every one who becomes a leader in fact. A person can act as a leader by advancing a definition of a public situation and a prescription for collective action to deal with it. But not unless he or she succeeds in mobilizing a following for the position thus taken does that individual *become* a leader. Although comparatively few do, the results are meaningful. Conventional political science more or less neglects the phenomenon of nonconstituted leadership because it considers politics to be about power only, and nonconstituted leaders, by definition, lack power. When and if they acquire it, they have transformed themselves into constituted leaders. Yet nonconstituted leadership is something that political science overlooks at its intellectual peril, because very much that is politically significant in the world thus remains outside its purview.

25. Andrei D. Sakharov, "A Sick Society," *The New York Times*, 23 January 1980.

How important nonconstituted leaders have been in past history, and may become in future history, will be made more clear in the remainder of this study. They typically emerge as leaders of sociopolitical movements.

3

Leadership through Social Movements

So far we have proceeded on the implicit assumption that when circumstances arouse the concern of sizable groups of people in a political community, constituted leadership diagnoses the problem situation involved and prescribes a policy response. But that assumption does not always hold true. Many sets of circumstances have meaningfully impinged upon the purposes and concerns of large numbers of people without being defined, at least for a long time, as problem situations about which political communities should take action. Historical examples would include slavery, serfdom, the lack of suffrage for women and the poor, minorities' deprivation of civil rights, extremes of poverty, child labor, and the danger of chemical pollution.

When constituted leadership fails to define meaningful circumstances as a situation calling for action, nonconstituted leadership may, at some point, start doing so. Individuals in the political community may independently diagnose heretofore accepted conditions as wrong and remediable. They may devise proposals for change and publicly urge their acceptance. Constituted political authority may not react positively to such initiatives, but numbers of people, especially from the group or groups directly affected by the circumstances in question, may respond, often eagerly, to the nonconstituted leaders' diagnoses and prescriptions for action. When that happens, movements for change arise. Insofar as they take part in and influence the political life of their societies, they merit the designation *sociopolitical*. If, as often happens, the movements become organized, the originally nonconstituted leaders typically acquire constituted leadership roles within the directing organizations of the movements. And if the movements acquire state power, as has often happened, they become constituted leaders of states. Guerrilla leaders assume presidencies, for example.

Sociopolitical movements for change are leadership phenomena in two related senses. First, they characteristically arise through leadership activity by individuals at a time when constituted authority is not providing leadership of their variety, but when receptivity to that type of leadership exists in the political community. Second, once in being, a sociopolitical movement can furnish leadership for change that is not being provided by constituted authority. Such leadership may or may not be successful. If successful, it may be so in different ways. It may, for example, succeed by provoking or pressuring constituted authority in the community to adopt, in some form or degree, the movement's diagnosis of the situation and its recipes for corrective action. Alternatively, it may carry through its program by acquiring state power, whether legally or through violent revolution, and therewith the capacity to act for change from constituted leadership positions.

Political science, in my view, has overconcentrated on the workings of established polities and given too little systematic attention to sociopolitical movements. One source of this deficiency lies in the failure to develop an analysis of the political process within which such movements find a logical and important place. Another is the already noted tendency of political scientists to see their topic as the study of power and the powerful and to focus primary attention upon the study of the state as the organization that—as Weber put it—monopolizes the legitimate use of coercion on a certain territory. Unless terrorist in their mode of operation, sociopolitical movements rarely possess much coercive power, and unless they become a government they may never monopolize it on a sizable territory.

Yet movements have played a remarkably large role in political history and continue to do so. Very many have captured power by revolutionary politics. Some, upon achieving power, have created what have been called "movement-regimes" that continue to pursue the politics of change from governmental positions. The roster of twentieth-century leaders whose names might not have bulked large in history but for their involvement in successful sociopolitical movements would include Lenin, Trotsky, Stalin, Mussolini, Hitler, Nehru, Nasser, Ben-Gurion, Nkrumah, Ben Bella, Castro, and de Gaulle. In many more cases, movements and their leaders have mattered in political life without forming governments.

From the leadership standpoint, the study of sociopolitical movements and their dynamics is integral to the study of the political process itself. Political science as "state science" is of necessity, therefore, critically incomplete.

Causes of Nondefinition

The study of movements for change properly begins with consideration of the conditions in which they arise. Our hypothesis is that they tend to arise when circumstances adversely affecting considerable numbers of people in a political community are going undefined as a problem situation by constituted political authority despite the possibility of change (which can mean anything from the circumstances' amelioration to their abolition) and when, as a result, no action is being taken for change.

Some among the many possible explanations of this phenomenon are especially noteworthy. First is time-honored usage or convention, often called *culture*. A society's culture, as an anthropologist describes it, is its customary, socially transmitted way of life, comprising both prevailing practices, or "real culture patterns," and prevailing norms, beliefs, and values, or "ideal culture patterns."[1] In any particular society at any given time, there will be greater or lesser discrepancies between real and ideal patterns, between the ways most people regularly behave and the ways they believe one ought to behave. Through socialization (or acculturation), the young are inducted into the culture by training and experience. They learn both the ideal culture patterns or accepted principles and, also, especially as they graduate into adulthood, the prevalent practices. Where discrepancies exist, socialization works toward training the new generation into acceptance of them. If slavery, for example, is an established set of practices in a particular society although incongruent with certain religious principles held by most people in that society, the generality of the society's members, slaves included, may be socialized into believing in the rightness of the institution so long as slaves are treated according to certain rules.

But human beings who have the opportunity to develop and realize their human potentialities are not fatally imprisoned by socialization into their society's culture.

1. According to Ralph Linton, a real culture pattern is "a limited range of behaviors within which the responses of a society's members to a particular situation will normally fall," and an ideal culture pattern is "the consensus of opinion on the part of the society's members as to how people should behave in particular situations." *The Cultural Background of Personality* (New York: Appleton-Century-Crofts), pp. 46, 52.

Many, it is true, grow up and remain conformists, but not all do. Through autonomous self-development some outgrow, transcend, and on occasion rebel against what psychologist Gordon Allport calls their "tribal codes," in other words, their culture.[2] In a slave-owning society, for example, some people eventually come to believe, contrary to their socialization, that slavery is wrong. Among these some may define slavery publicly as a problem situation and call for emancipation as the policy response. If others follow their lead, an abolitionist movement emerges.

One possible avenue of escape from the socialization that one receives in one's own culture is access to another culture whose ways of living and believing differ from those learned at home. Some persons socialized into one culture may be exposed to a different one by travel or study abroad and be influenced by its ways. Alternatively, a person may "visit" via books a culture distant from him in space or time. An exemplar of escape from home culture through foreign study is the eighteenth-century Russian, Alexander Radishchev. Russia was then an agrarian society whose economy was based on serfdom in a form hardly distinguishable from slavery for a large portion of the peasant population. Radishchev was one of the highborn young Russians who went abroad for advanced education. In Leipzig University, where he studied between 1766 and 1771, he came under the influence of French Enlightenment thought. Later he was inspired by the American Revolution. He became a passionate opponent of serfdom. In the 1780s he wrote an antiserfdom tract, *Journey from Petersburg to Moscow*. With the help of friends, he produced 650 copies of it on his own printing

2. Gordon W. Allport, *Becoming: Basic Considerations for a Psychology of Personality* (New Haven: Yale University Press, 1955), p. 71.

machine. Some were sold in a bookstore. For this crime he was condemned to death. Empress Catherine, who directed the investigation of the case, commuted the sentence to ten years of Siberian exile. From a leadership standpoint, the *Journey* was Radishchev's definition of the Russian serfdom situation as intolerable, from which it followed that the serfs should be freed. No antiserfdom movement emerged, however. It is interesting to compare his attempt at nonconstituted leadership and its fate with that of Harriet Beecher Stowe, a nonconstituted leader of the American abolitionist movement. Her *Uncle Tom's Cabin*, a definition of the American slavery situation as intolerable, published in book form in 1852, is reckoned among the causes of the Civil War.

The cultural conformity that militates against the recognition of problem situations on the part of constituted authority may be powerfully reinforced by the economic self-interest of a dominant social group—such as pre-Reform Russia's serf-owning nobility and Antebellum America's slave-owning class—in preserving things as they are. For example, before its recent transition to black rule as Zimbabwe, Rhodesia was a country where 6 million blacks were dominated by 270,000 whites under a government that ruled on behalf of the white minority. Sir Roy Welensky, who was prime minister of Rhodesia from 1956 to 1963 and saw the necessity for eventual transition to black rule, explained the white minority's resistance to change by saying, "People have two motor cars, servants, swimming pools, a nice house. The cost of living is cheap. Look how pleasant life is here for the white people. It's died everywhere else, but it survives here, and people don't want to lose that way of life, do they?"[3] From the standpoint of the white-minority gov-

3. *The New York Times*, 30 June 1976.

ernment (prior to the outside-mediated transition), the problem situation was not the established practice of white domination but rather the blacks' efforts to change things through a liberation movement. Just so, the circumstance that Empress Catherine defined as a problem situation was not the serf culture but rather Radishchev's outraged protest against it, and her policy response as a constituted leader was, logically, the punishment of the offender.

Repression, which can be seen as leadership for nonchange, is commonly a complacent society's response to difficult conditions that the dominant minority or majority does not wish to recognize as a problem situation save insofar as people protest against them or strive, through a movement, to change them. Cultural conformism, economic self-interest, and the wish for an untroubled conscience can intermingle as motivations here. All these are involved in an example eloquently discussed by the Bronx borough commander of the New York City Police Department, Anthony V. Bouza, in a published interview. There exists in America, he points out, a ghetto subculture of unemployment, alcoholism, drugs, and violence. This is a set of circumstances that America does not define as a problem situation because of unwillingness to take the costly remedial measures that would be needed to resolve the problem:

> America attacks the problems that it sees. It doesn't see these problems. . . . There hasn't been a significant redistribution of income in this nation for 30 years. The bureaucracy and the government are failing and fundamentally the federal government has simply got to look at what is happening in the city ghetto and address it. To the degree that I succeed in keeping the ghetto cool, to the degree that I can be effective—to that degree, fundamentally, am I deflecting America's attention from discovering this can-

cer? . . . The fact of the matter is that we are manufacturing criminals. . . . We are very efficiently creating a very volatile and dangerous sub-element of our society. And we are doing it simply because we don't want to face the burdens and the problems and the responsibilities that their existence imposes on any society with conscience.

Acting as a leader by incisively defining the situation that American society and its constituted authority have neglected to define—save as a problem of violence, for which policing is the policy response—officer Bouza concludes that he is very well paid "almost to be the commander of an army of occupation in the ghetto. And that is a real tragedy, I think."[4] At least implicitly, he was urging upon American society the need for a movement to change and ultimately abolish the ghetto subculture. As of this time of writing, there has been no serious response.

Still another force for nondefinition is general ignorance of circumstances that would, if known, take on sufficiently acute meaning for large numbers of people that their existence *would* be defined as a problem. We have noted such a case in the previous chapter. Before the publication of Carson's *Silent Spring*, the American public was largely unaware of the dangers inherent in uncontrolled use of chemical pesticides. The facts, she claimed, were known to the producers of the pesticides and to the control men in government. But in the interests of business as usual, they were keeping quiet about them. Her signalizing of the circumstances and her diagnosing of the danger they represent helped end public ignorance and thereby fostered emergence of the American ecological movement.

4. Anthony V. Bouza, "A Tough Job That Raises Hard Questions," *The Philadelphia Inquirer*, 18 August 1978. See also Joseph D. McNamara, "'Schools' for Crime," *The New York Times*, 24 October 1980. Mr. McNamara is chief of police in San Jose, California.

I have argued that movements for change tend to arise when leadership by constituted authority is in default, that is, when circumstances exist that could or should be defined as a problem situation for the political community but are not; or when the leadership shown by constituted authority is negative in the sense that what is seen as the problem is the very effort of people to treat certain circumstances as a problem so that something may be done to change them. But it has also happened that constituted authority offers positive leadership in troubled conditions, without serious effect, and a movement for change arises with a definition of the situation that proves effective, in part, because it focuses upon circumstances that do not exist—but in which people are willing to believe. A historic case involving such fictitious circumstances, German National Socialism, will be examined below.

How Movements Arise

Social scientists sometimes discuss movements without emphasizing the role that leadership normally plays in their inception. Thus, a sociologist writes, "A social movement occurs when a fairly large number of people band together in order to alter or supplant some portion of the existing culture or social order."[5] This description fails to bring out the dynamics involved in the formation of social movements. The question is, when *do* people band together for such purposes, and how does the process typically take place?

It is my contention that it typically occurs through successful leadership activity of a sort not being undertaken by constituted authority. A person or persons show

5. William Bruce Cameron, *Modern Social Movements* (New York: Random House, 1966), p. 7.

initiative as nonconstituted leaders along some path not being taken by constituted authority. They define a set of circumstances that deeply concern people as an urgent problem situation, or—if that has been done already by others, in or out of government—they define the situation in a novel way. They propose a course of collective action to meet the situation as defined. And they seek the support of others for their view of what the situation is and what should be done about it. If they succeed in all this, if people respond to their diagnosis and their plan of action, a movement begins to form.

What determines their success or failure in rallying sufficient support to start a movement? Among the obvious determinants are: the depth and breadth of the concern that exists in the political community over the circumstances in question; the cogency of the newly proffered diagnosis of the situation and proposed plan of action to the minds of people directly affected by the circumstances; the degree to which constituted authority is showing some leadership on its own part in the matter; and the presence or absence in the society of the freedoms of speech, press, and organizing that are requisite for the unhampered development of a social movement. Depending chiefly on these factors and their interrelationship, a movement may remain small and on the fringes of society, may grow to larger size, or may become so large that it merits the name *mass movement*.

Once a movement starts, an organization usually emerges to give it direction, and those who initiated the movement as nonconstituted leaders become the constituted leaders of it. Alternatively, a small organizational base, oftentimes in the form of a political party, may antedate the movement's growth to sizable proportions. Organizational structure, doctrine, ideology, ritual, on occasion uniforms and insignia, and in general all that can be summed up under the heading of the movement's *culture* make their appearance. But in the beginning is the leadership act. A "leaderless movement" is virtually out of the question. It could only mean a movement in which all of the members acted as leaders in unison.

Two historical cases illustrate these points. One is the Townsend Plan movement in America; the other is the Nazi movement in Germany.

At the depth of the Great Depression in 1933, a country doctor from North Dakota, Francis E. Townsend, was living in California retirement and trying to make a living in real estate. One morning he looked out his window and saw three old women rummaging in garbage cans for edible scraps. Not far away, he saw store windows filled with food. The contrast aroused in him a wave of moral indignation that did not subside under the effort of Mrs. Townsend to calm him down. Incensed, he wanted the whole nation to hear how he felt about these conditions, which he knew were widespread in depression-stricken America.[6]

Out of his indignation and the resulting thought process came an act of leadership that made Dr. Townsend the nationally known leader of a mass movement. He devised a plan for action in the situation that he had diagnosed as wrong but remediable, and he presented his plan in a letter sent to newspaper editors across the country. This letter recounted the scene he had witnessed and proposed a course of action aimed at relieving widespread poverty in the midst of American plenty and spurring economic recovery in the process. A tax of 2 percent would be levied on all business transactions. All citizens aged sixty or over would receive a monthly pension of two

6. My discussion of the Townsend Plan movement is based on the detailed account in Hadley Cantril, *The Psychology of Social Movements* (New York: John Wiley & Sons, 1963), chap. 7.

hundred dollars and would agree under oath to spend this money within the U.S. borders in thirty days' time. The letter offered a vision of the benefits that would result. Older people would live in dignity. Jobs would become available for the young. Prosperity would revive in the nation, the crime rate and taxes would go down, and the budget would come into balance.

The letter sparked a movement. Scores of newspapers printed it, thousands of people responded. Officially inaugurated on New Year's Day of 1934 by Dr. Townsend and other nonconstituted leaders who had joined him, the movement spread very rapidly. An organization was set up, financed by a membership fee of twenty-five cents a year, in return for which each member received a pamphlet describing the plan and urging him or her to form a Townsend club locally. Four thousand clubs, averaging five hundred members each, were reportedly in existence by late 1935. Petitions weighing thousands of pounds were sent to Congress. A new organization, the Townsend National Legion, was formed, with dues of one dollar monthly. There were Townsend buttons bearing the motto, Youth for Work—Age for Leisure. Speakers were sent out to ask older people how they would like to spend their proposed pensions. Dr. Townsend flew around the country by airplane, making personal appearances at huge picnics attended by as many as thirty thousand people. A campaign was launched to attract members among the young and middle-aged as well as among the elderly. By the fall of 1935, the movement was well enough organized to stage a national political convention.

The mobilizing of support went on in all these ways. Yet no energetic membership drive could have produced such spectacular results but for the eager receptivity of hundreds of thousands of distressed elderly Americans to

Dr. Townsend's leadership act—his definition of their situation as intolerable but remediable, and his proposal for improving it. Although the plan was not realized, the movement helped foster the political atmosphere in which social security and other New Deal reforms were enacted. As these relieved the privation to which the plan was addressed, the movement waned in the later 1930s. Its success in contributing to distress-relieving change was its undoing as a movement.

The Townsend Plan movement quite clearly exhibits the dynamics of sociopolitical movements as leadership phenomena. German National Socialism is a more complex case in which the nonconstituted leadership activity that fostered the movement was not, as with Dr. Townsend, morally benign. The Nazi movement arose in the aftermath of the First World War, when Germany was afflicted by the dislocations of war and the trauma of defeat. It was born in the beer halls of Munich, the capital of Bavaria, a province then the scene of much revolutionary and counterrevolutionary extremism. The ex-soldier Adolf Hitler moved as an agitator (a "drummer," he later called himself) among groups of disgruntled and demoralized war veterans and others potentially receptive to his nationalist-racist message. One of numerous such would-be leaders, he was distinguished by extraordinary oral persuasive powers deriving from fanatical conviction. His message, briefly, was that Germany's and the world's present troubles were the result of a "Jewish-Marxist world conspiracy" (his phrase). The Jews, whom he described in a written political statement of September 1919 as the "racial tuberculosis of nations," were responsible for Germany's shame and misery. Having so defined the situation, he prescribed a course of action for dealing with it: creation of a government of national power whose ultimate goal "must absolutely be the removal of the Jews altogether."[7] That document prefigured the genocidal "final solution."

As Germany's distress deepened owing to economic crisis and catastrophic inflation, which were aggravated by France's military occupation of the Ruhr at the outset of 1923, Hitler acquired a mass following. People flocked to him "as to a Saviour," according to a contemporary report. The membership of the National Socialist party—the movement's organizational base—increased by some thirty-five thousand between February and November of 1923.[8] In November, Hitler organized a putsch in Munich, hoping to take power locally preparatory to a march on Berlin. The move failed. He was arrested, tried, and sentenced to a term in the Landsberg fortress-prison outside Munich. While there he wrote part one of *Mein Kampf*.

In form autobiographical, in substance this book was a five-hundred-page elaboration of the diagnosis of the situation offered in his speeches at mass rallies and in party proclamations. The troubles and suffering of Germany, the world, and the Aryan race were put down to a satanic conspiracy by international Jewry to achieve world domination by a variety of stealthy means, ranging from the pollution of Aryan blood to control of the press and subversion of states by Marxism, which Hitler presented as a Jewish machination. He supported the diagnosis by referring to a document, "The Protocols of the Elders of Zion." This tract, which originated in Russia early in the twentieth century, is a forgery. It purports to be an account of a secret meeting of Jewish elders, in 1897, the year of the convening of the first Zionist Congress, and their plot to undermine society, overthrow gov-

7. Joachim Fest, *Hitler*, trans. Richard and Clara Winston (New York: Random House, 1975), pp. 113, 115.
8. Ibid., pp. 154, 162.

ernments, destroy Christianity, and enslave the world to the Jews.[9] Hitler dismissed press claims that the document was spurious. Whether or not he personally believed in its authenticity, he was obsessed by the idea of a Jewish conspiracy to rule the world.

Here was the most consequential twentieth-century case in which a movement leader's definition of a situation rested on a combination of real and fictitious circumstances. The real ones were the troubles Germany was experiencing when Hitler appeared before mass audiences in the early 1920s and wrote his book: desperate material hardship, widespread disorientation and demoralization, anxiety over the future of self and family, a national sense of humiliation over a lost war and resulting reparations, the presence to the east of a Soviet Russia professing Marxism and seeing in Germany a likely center of European revolution, and so on. The Jewish-Marxist conspiracy was, on the other hand, unreal, a fictitious circumstance, though not seen as such by Hitler and many of his associates in the movement. It was the mixture of the real and the fictitious (but credible to many) circumstances that imparted to Hitler's diagnosis of Germany's situation its explosive power as a leadership formula compared to what Germans were then hearing from their constituted leaders.

As a rule, it has been noted earlier, political leaders include in their diagnoses of public problem situations some explanation of the circumstances arousing concern, since the persuasiveness of their proposed policy response will normally turn on the credibility of their view of the

9. For Hitler's use of the document, see Adolf Hitler, *Mein Kampf* (New York: Reynal & Hitchcock, 1939), pp. 423–24. On the history and political uses of the forgery, see Norman Cohn, *Warrant for Genocide: The Myth of the Jewish World Conspiracy and the Protocols of the Elders of Zion* (London: Eyre, 1967).

problem's underlying sources. When distress is extreme and its causation mysterious, as was the case in the Germany of that time, reasoned analysis of problems' sources, such as the authorities were offering, could not easily compete in the larger public arena with the Nazis' version. To the confused, disappointed, perplexed, and fearful, of whom there were very many, this version offered a simple explanation of circumstances otherwise beyond their comprehension; and the anti-Semitism latent in the national culture made the simple explanation all the more beguiling. The theme of the world Jewish conspiracy drew everything together, made all sorts of painful common experiences suddenly understandable. It identified an outside cause for both individual and national problems and prescribed a fight against a cunning evil enemy as the logical response. Solving one's own problems by combating other people said to be the cause of them was alluring to many, all the more so as the malaise was deep and its causation dark.

Here a comparison with reported experiences of persons who gravitate to paranoid solutions may be useful. Harry Stack Sullivan writes that what is crucial in the paranoid dynamism is the "transference of blame" and that this typically comes about in a moment of intense illumination. The person will often report, "And then I saw it all!" Sullivan goes on: "And the great thing is that finally a happy hypothesis has been received into awareness: It is not that I have something wrong with me, but that *he* does something to me. One is the victim, not of one's own defects, but of a devilish environment. One is not to blame; the environment is to blame."[10] Hitler was addressing himself to Germans who, though doubtless not clinically paranoid in their vast majority, were victims in

10. Harry Stack Sullivan, *Clinical Studies in Psychiatry* (New York: W. W. Norton, 1956), p. 146.

various senses, and he was identifying a particular sort of devilish environment as the agent of their misfortunes. Having himself "seen it all" at some point in his life, he strove with all his might to make them see it too, and many in his mass audiences (few seem to have read his long book) appear to have experienced the stark clarification that he communicated.

But it was only the factual reality of acute distress, the actual circumstances of want, insecurity, and meaninglessness, that made Germans in large numbers receptive to Hitler's diagnosis of fictional circumstances as the source of the nation's problems, and to his prescription of a national revolution under his leadership as the guarantee of a solution. Accordingly, the fortunes of his movement rose and fell with the distress level in Germany. Having grown as the economic crisis deepened in 1921–1923, his following shrank as conditions improved afterward. Then, in the Great Depression, when the number of Germany's unemployed increased to 3 million by September 1930, the Nazi party's vote leaped from a previous 810,000 to 6.4 million in that year's national election. In the election of July 1932, at which time the number of jobless stood at an intolerable 5 to 6 million, the Nazis emerged as the strongest party in the Reichstag.[11] Now Hitler was in a position to bluster and maneuver his way to power, as he did in the ensuing months. Needless to add, such further factors as the Nazis' organizational and agitational tactics, monetary support from worried conservatives, and the ineffectiveness of moderate leadership contributed to the outcome.

Sociopolitical movements are a characteristic, though not invariable and exclusive, habitat of what, following

11. Fest, *Hitler*, pp. 269, 287, 332. Fest writes: "There is no question that Hitler's effectiveness was entirely bound up with national distress" (p. 180).

the usage of Max Weber, is called "charismatic" leadership. A charismatic leader, according to Weber, is one who arouses fervent loyalty and devotion, even worship, among the followers.[12] Why leaders of movements for change would often be the objects of such loyalty and enthusiasm is understandable: the leader, by virtue of personal attributes combined with the diagnosis of the situation as wrong but remediable and the formula for remedying it, embodies in the minds of distressed followers the promise of salvation from distress, a way out of the impasse that confronts them and the society. In short, a charismatic leader is one perceived by the followers as a savior, a messiah.

Some dissatisfaction with existing conditions is the normal motivation for joining or supporting a sociopolitical movement for change. If dissatisfaction is extreme, it falls in the category of distress. Thus not all movement leaders are charismatic, if only because not all followings are dissatisfied to the point of actual distress. But when they are, and when the movement leader signifies salvation to the followers' minds, the charismatic response will appear. Considering how often in history movements have enlisted the deeply distressed, it is plain why they are a characteristic habitat of charisma.

We see this phenomenon in both of the movements whose rise has been examined here. In the case of Dr. Townsend, the charismatic appeal appears to have had little to do with qualities of personality or oratory and everything to do with the simple cogency of his diagnosis of the situation and his plan for alleviating it. He was not a colorful leader-personality. He reportedly spoke in a

12. For a full discussion of Weber's position, the literature about charismatic leadership, and an interpretation of the concept, which I here briefly summarize, see Robert C. Tucker, "The Theory of Charismatic Leadership," *Daedalus* 97: 3 (Summer 1968): 731–56.

"dry flat voice." Yet at the height of the movement he was a shining figure in the eyes of his followers. At club meetings he was regularly referred to as "that great humanitarian" and a man "truly inspired by God." After the movement became organized, his lieutenants capitalized upon his charisma to establish a Townsend personality cult. The movement's national *Weekly*, for example, adopted as one of its slogans, The Three Emancipators— Washington, Lincoln, Townsend. An official song began, "Onward Townsend soldiers, marching as to war, with the Townsend banner going on before."[13]

In Hitler's case the evidence of charismatic appeal is abundant, especially at the time of Germany's most acute distress. Thus, after a meeting attended by 120,000 people in 1932, a Hamburg schoolteacher reported scenes of "moving faith" in which Hitler appeared "as the helper, rescuer, redeemer from overwhelming need."[14] But Hitler's charisma did not derive, as Townsend's did, simply from his way of defining the national crisis situation and prescribing a remedy for it. The intensity of his oratory, which again and again whipped the mass audiences into a frenzy, was an additional factor of importance, and underlying it all was his own passionate belief in himself as the hero-savior of the nation that his devoted followers took him to be. Little by little, the movement's organization, with his active encouragement, consciously institutionalized his charisma in a Hitler personality cult that became a hallmark of Nazi culture.

Although frequently found in movements for the reason given above, charismatic leadership is by no means confined to that setting. Insofar as political leaders who are not movement leaders come to power in times of dis-

13. See Cantril, *Psychology of Social Movements*, for the factual particulars mentioned here.
14. Fest, *Hitler*, p. 328.

tress in their political communities and embody the promise of relief, either because of their ways of defining the situation and prescribing a solution or by such qualities of personality as the power to communicate confidence, or by both in combination, they appear charismatic to their followings. Notable examples are Winston Churchill as the defiant war leader of Britain in her time of greatest national danger in 1940 and the Franklin Roosevelt who told Americans at the worst point in the Great Depression that they had nothing to fear but fear itself and presided over a government acting in ways that bore his words out.

Because the phenomenon of charisma turns on the felt presence of serious distress, a movement's or a leader's success in fulfilling the promise of relief can result in the decline and fall of charisma. A leader, in other words, may be charismatic for followers at one time and not at another when their distress, for whatever combination of reasons, has been substantially relieved. Thus, Churchill was no longer charismatic for most Britons when the Second World War ended and lost power with his party in the early postwar national elections. By the end of the 1930s, when economic conditions had considerably improved for most Americans, Roosevelt remained broadly popular but hardly charismatic. An institutionalized personality cult can continue to give a leader the appearance of being charismatic when in fact he is not. Because it does not reflect the real feelings of followers toward a leader, such a cult can be described as pseudocharisma. This often manifests itself in authoritarian political systems, in which a regime's monopoly of the media of public communication makes possible a continuing show of largely unfelt adulation.

For purposes of analysis, sociopolitical movements may be divided into two broad categories: movements for reform and movements for revolution. In what follows I wish to consider first the one and then the other from the standpoint of leadership. Each of the two types of movements has its characteristic way of defining the situation and prescribing change.

Leadership for Reform

Reform politics is broader than movement politics. Reform leaders have often appeared as heads of government or in other constituted roles of leadership, such as legislative or judicial posts, and have furnished leadership for reform without initiating political movements. In other cases, however, of which Roosevelt's New Deal administration may offer an illustration, constituted leadership can generate something resembling a reform movement.

Reform politics is perhaps as diverse in motivation as in manifestation. No single characteristic motive for reform leadership can be specified. It may be a moral belief, a power drive, or a search for glory. It may be a complex combination of these, which appears to have been the case with Woodrow Wilson as a reform leader in the presidency of Princeton, the governorship of New Jersey, and the presidency of the United States. Still another possible motivation is pragmatic concern for the continued stability of a political order that would be endangered by failure to change certain conditions.

When, for example, Alexander II assumed the throne of Russia in 1855 following the long, repressive reign of his father, "Iron Czar" Nicholas I, and in the midst of a losing war in the Crimea that dramatized Russia's backwardness vis-à-vis her adversaries, France and Great Britain, the new czar defined Russia's situation in terms of the urgent need for modernizing reforms starting with the emancipation of the serfs. Moral considerations may also have influenced him, for he told the novelist Ivan Turgenev that he had been impressed by the latter's *Sportsman's Sketches*, a book about rural Russia that carried strong abolitionist overtones. Early in 1856, Alexander told assembled representatives of the Moscow nobility, "It is better to abolish serfdom from above than to await the time when it will begin to abolish itself from below. I request you, gentlemen, to consider how this may be achieved."[15] The situation was thus diagnosed as one of urgent pragmatic need for a far-reaching reform in order to forestall a revolutionary upheaval that would otherwise be likely. The outcome was the Emancipation Decree of 1861, which inaugurated a series of further reforms that, together with the abolition of serfdom, changed much in Russian society without, however, dismantling the autocratic, centralized, and bureaucratic system of government.

For various reasons, as noted above, conditions that arouse deep and anguished concern in many people, as serfdom did in Russia, can long go undiagnosed by constituted political authority as a problem situation calling for remedial action. It may be the concern itself, or overt expression of it, as in Radishchev's *Journey from Petersburg to Moscow*, that official leadership sees as the problem and seeks to solve by repressive means. In historical contexts of this kind, we have hypothesized, some individuals may act as nonconstituted leaders in ways that spark sociopolitical movements for change. In many instances, these are reform movements.

Leaders of reform movements have a characteristic way of defining the collective situation. To their minds, it

15. W. E. Mosse, *Alexander II and the Modernization of Russia*, rev. ed. (New York: Collier Books, 1962), pp. 41–42. For Alexander's remark to Turgenev, see p. 41.

presents a wrong and remediable discrepancy between the political community's principles (its "ideal culture patterns," to revert to Linton's terminology) and its customary practices, its "real culture patterns," or some particular set of them. We have noted that discrepancies of this kind commonly exist in political communities; they may be glaring. Thus it may be an accepted article of belief that citizens should have the right to vote, but in practice some section of the population, such as women or members of a minority group, may be deprived of voting ability. The principle of equality before the law may coexist with various forms of inequality in practice. Through socialization, especially as they move into the adult world, most individuals learn to take the discrepancies for granted; and special patterns of belief often evolve in support of them. For example, the set of real culture patterns in South Africa termed *apartheid*, although in conflict with certain ethico-religious principles professed by many South African whites, is backed by the principles of a special apartheid doctrine also professed by many of these same people.

A proposition must be added now to the analysis of a sociocultural system offered by Linton. A human society is something beyond the total complex of ideal and real culture patterns constituting a community's way of life and thought, even when allowance has been made for the existence of subcultures. There is always a core belief, a central motif, in which the ideal culture patterns are embedded, and I propose to call this the society's *sustaining myth*. The term *myth* is not being used here in the frequently encountered derogatory sense in which it means an untruth. Such myths are the sources in which people find meaning in membership in their society; thus, in a manner of speaking, the myths *are* the society as a mental fact. A sustaining myth is a notion or concept of that society as a common enterprise. It represents what is distinctively valuable about the society from the standpoint of its members. America, for example, might be characterized, in terms of its sustaining myth, as a community of free and equal self-governing citizens pursuing their individual ends in a spirit of tolerance for their religious and other forms of diversity.

With some individuals, the socialization processes that dispose persons to live in peace with discordances between ideal and real culture patterns, and especially between their society's sustaining myth (in their understanding of it) and prevalent practices, do not work effectively. Precisely because the sustaining myth is deeply meaningful to them, the clash of certain practices with it comes to seem intolerable. These are persons of what we may describe as the "reform mentality." They are inclined to define the rift between principle and practice, between the society's sustaining myth and the ways in which some members of it are behaving toward other members, as a wrong situation that can and should be eliminated by *altering the practices in question*. They became abolitionists of slavery, fighters for suffrage for groups of the population that are denied voting rights, seekers of change in the big-city ghetto conditions that breed crime and violence, and so forth. They devise ways of dramatizing the issue and of persuading people, or the government perhaps, to change established patterns of action or inaction.

If these leadership activities elicit a considerable public response, a reform movement comes into existence. Those who give it active support will, in many cases, be persons whose concern over the practices to which the leader objects is not hard to arouse because these practices cause them grief, perhaps by injuring their dignity, perhaps by restricting their career opportunities, perhaps by denying them work or keeping them in poverty. Some who join the movement, however, will be non-disadvantaged individuals moved by moral commitment. If the movement grows and shows signs of success, still others may become active in it for self-seeking motives. To paraphrase what Crane Brinton said of revolutionaries in *The Anatomy of Revolution*, it takes almost as many kinds of people to make a movement for change as it does to make a world.

Dr. Martin Luther King, Jr., is a notable exemplar of the reform leader in recent American history, and the civil-rights movement in which he became prominent exemplifies the phenomenon of reform movements. The phase in which King became active as a leader started in Montgomery, Alabama, on 1 December 1955, when a black woman, Rosa Parks, refused a bus driver's order to move to the rear of the bus in accordance with the then prevalent practice of segregated seating arrangements. Mrs. Parks was arrested for violating Montgomery's segregation ordinances. King, then pastor of a local Baptist church, joined with other leaders of Montgomery's black community in defining those circumstances as a wrong situation that could and should be corrected. In response they proclaimed a Montgomery bus boycott as a nonviolent form of mass opposition to bus segregation. An earlier study of Gandhism, in 1950, had helped to incline King's mind toward the tactics of nonviolently confronting upholders of practices deviant from America's professed principles; and the wrongness of segregation in principle had been declared by the U.S. Supreme Court when, on 31 May 1955, it ordered school desegregation "with all deliberate speed." King's role of leadership in the ensuing 382-day Montgomery bus boycott, which was supported by the local black citizens en masse, propelled him to national prominence as a leader of the civil-rights movement.[16]

That King was a man of reform mentality is clear from his pronouncements in the antidiscrimination movement. This mentality spoke, for example, in his letter from the Birmingham, Alabama, jail, in which he said, "One day the South will know that when these disinherited children of God sat down at lunch counters they were in reality standing up for the best in the American dream and the most sacred values in our Judeo-Christian heritage, and thus carrying our whole nation back to great wells of democracy which were dug deep by the founding fathers in the formulation of the Constitution and the Declaration of Independence."[17] King was recalling Americans to the ideal culture patterns laid down in the charter documents of their democracy. He was protesting the deviation of some practices from American society's sustaining myth as he understood and professed it.

Reformers are characteristically outraged by contradictions between what their political community professes and some of the practices it condones. But effective leaders of reform mentality are rarely persons in whom anger is the salient emotion. They typically possess and can persuasively convey to others a vision of what the society would be like, how it would look, *if* its ideals were

16. This summary of the facts follows the account given by Lerone Bennett, Jr., in "When the Man and the Hour Are Met," in *Martin Luther King, Jr.: A Profile*, ed. C. Eric Lincoln (New York: Hill and Wang, 1970), pp. 7–39.

17. Cited by Haig Bosmajian, "The Letter from Birmingham Jail," in ibid., p. 136. In "The Conservative Militant," his contribution to this collection, August Meyer writes that King "was capitalizing on the basic consensus of values in American society by awakening the conscience of the white man to the contradiction between his professions and the facts of discrimination" (p. 153).

realized in practice. Such a vision of community was notable in King. He kept referring to the "dream" and the "American dream." This was a vision of American society as it would be if its sustaining myth were lived up to by all. His dream America contained, too, the vision of a new black community within American society. This was expressed in a Montgomery sermon in which he said to the people assembled in the church, "If you will protest courageously, and yet with dignity and Christian love, when the history books are written in future generations, the historians will have to pause and say, 'There lived a great people—a black people—who injected new meaning and dignity into the veins of civilization.'"[18] The mobilizing power of such a vision, so communicated, was shown in King's tragically shortened career as a reform leader.

Not always does attempted reform leadership, whether by a constituted or a nonconstituted leader, result in the rise of a reform movement. For various reasons, the recall to a political community's ideal culture patterns may not evoke a strong enough or wide enough response to generate a movement of opposition to deviant real patterns. For a case in point, we may refer to Russia after Stalin, where a constituted leader, Nikita Khrushchev, then first secretary of the Soviet Communist party, delivered, on the night of 24–25 February 1956, before a closed session of the Twentieth Party Congress, a denunciation of his predecessor, Stalin, for having systematically violated the Communist party's "holy Leninist principles" during many years by abandoning the "Leninist method of convincing and educating" in favor of "administrative violence, mass repressions and terror."[19]

18. Lerone Bennett, in ibid., p. 17.
19. Khrushchev's secret speech, which has been published abroad but not in the USSR, was entitled "On the Cult of Personality and Its Consequences." An annotated text is available under the title "Crimes

No serious reform movement ensued in Soviet society. The reasons would include the secrecy of the proceedings, the effort to contain the reform impetus within the confines of the ruling party, and, not least, the fact that Stalin's mass repressions and terror had exterminated virtually an entire earlier generation of *believing* Communists, so that Khrushchev's party associates were, in their great majority, Stalin's creatures and not likely to be responsive to the call to condemn practices of an era that had been formative in their political lives. Nor did the forthright attempts of some surviving Communist believers to carry forward and broaden the leadership for reform, as nonconstituted leaders, bear fruit. For example, Roy A. Medvedev, who produced a vast enlargement of Khrushchev's indictment in a thousand-page tract called *Let History Judge: The Origins and Consequences of Stalinism*, which could not be published in Russia, was expelled from party membership for his pains. All this suggests that when deviations from professed principle have become a deep-rooted system over a long period, reform leadership may be ineffectual because the norms to which it would appeal have ceased to be meaningful enough to make reform politically feasible.

Reform leadership might seem, almost by definition, nonconservative because it is leadership for change, and conservatism is often viewed as an attitude of opposition to change. Yet conservatism has more than one meaning. It may mean attachment to the sociopolitical status quo, comprising both the generally accepted norms and the complex of prevailing practices. Discrepancies between the one and the other may be ignored, or they may be rationalized in a variety of ways. Another possible mean-

---

of the Stalin Era," in *The New Leader*, 16 July 1956. The words here cited appear on pp. S15 and S19 of that text.

ing of conservatism, however, is attachment to the political community's sustaining myth and ideal culture patterns as its foundation, its real constitution (whether or not set forth in a constitutional document). Reform leadership, which status-quo conservatives may see as dangerously radical, is in fact conservative in this latter sense: it would make ideal culture patterns practically more meaningful at the expense of making changes in the ways in which people, or some people, factually behave. Insofar as reform leadership and the movements it generates are effective, moreover, the consequence may be to consolidate a social order whose stability would be threatened by failure to confront and reduce the gap between ideals and everyday realities. That is why the true revolutionary almost always fears the reformer as one who, underneath it all, is a conservative enemy of the revolutionary cause.

Revolutionary Leadership

The revolutionary and the reformer both seek social change. One possible basis for distinguishing the one from the other is tactics. The reformer, it could be argued, characteristically seeks change by gradual and peaceful tactics that emphasize persuasion, whereas the revolutionary seeks change by extremist tactics that include violence. But there are objections to this reasoning. First, revolutionaries often adopt reformist tactics for a particular purpose at a given period, preparatory to the use of extreme means when conditions are ripe. In *Left-Wing Communism: An Infantile Disorder*, Lenin lectured the Communists of the world on the necessity of such flexibility. Second, some reform leaders, even though they eschew and abhor violence, have adopted tactics of nonviolent confrontation to which upholders of established

105

practices will predictably respond violently. Such was the case with Gandhi's march to the sea in the Salt Campaign of 1930, and again with peaceful civil-rights demonstrations that took place under the leadership of Martin Luther King. So, just as revolutionary politics may adopt reformist tactics for a particular time and purpose, reform politics may use nonviolent tactics that the reform leaders know are likely to provoke violence and thereby dramatize for the political community at large the very situation to whose presence they desire to call general attention.

Leadership for reform and leadership for revolution are best differentiated according to their divergent ways of apprehending and defining the collective situation. The reform leader, we have suggested, espouses the political community's sustaining myth, its professed ideal culture patterns, and defines the deviation of certain practices from those patterns as a wrong situation that can and should be corrected by changing the practices. Revolutionary leadership, on the other hand, sees and defines the collective situation as so irremediably wrong that the only possible solution is a fundamental reconstitution of society.

Revolutionary consciousness begins in estrangement, in a person's feeling of not being a part of the existing society, of not sharing its sustaining myth. The ideal as well as the real culture patterns are rejected. Indeed the former, along with the sustaining myth, will be the object of the revolutionary's special scorn because, as he sees it, the function of the myth and of the ideals is ideological—to obfuscate the realities of the collective situation by giving people the illusion that it is remediable. In seeking to mobilize a movement, therefore, a revolutionary leader will be particularly concerned to break the hold of the society's proclaimed principles upon the minds of people in the movement's hoped-for constituency.

As much as the reform leader, the revolutionary leader is possessed of a vision. But whereas the reformer's vision is of present society as it would be if its sustaining myth were made real, or more real, in the lives of its members, the revolutionary has a vision of a society founded on radically different principles. A revolutionary mind of great creative power will be one that forms or adumbrates a new concept of social living that may, if a revolution takes place, become the sustaining myth of a new society. The radically different principles advanced by a revolutionary leader may be past ones that have been forsaken, for example the principles of a true Islamic society as envisaged by the Iranian religious revolutionary Ayatollah Khomeini. Alternatively, they may be principles conceived and presented as unprecedented in human experience.

An archetypal revolutionary leader in the modern age, with an archetypal revolutionary mind, is Karl Marx. The *Communist Manifesto* of 1848 is his and Friedrich Engels's classic concise public presentation of their position and played a part in creating the most influential socialist movements of the nineteenth and twentieth centuries. Let us examine it not simply as the statement about past, present, and future history that it appears to be, but as a leadership act, a document that sought to perform the diagnostic, action-prescribing, and support-mobilizing functions of leadership as analyzed in the present study.

The meaningful circumstances that the *Manifesto* diagnoses as a problem situation are experiences that were widely endured by the industrial working class, or proletariat, during the Industrial Revolution and after: subsistence-level wages, inhumanly long working days, terrible working conditions, child labor, pauperism, ruined families, and despoiled lives. The *Manifesto*'s proffered definition of the collective situation explains those circumstances of working-class misery by the dynamics of capitalist production through exploitation of wage labor. It follows for Marx and Engels that the proletariat cannot end its misery by any other means than revolutionary mass action to overthrow the system that causes the misery. On this basis they prescribe proletarian class war against the bourgeoisie as the collective response to the situation. "The proletarians have nothing to lose but their chains," concludes the *Manifesto*. "They have a world to win. WORKING MEN OF ALL COUNTRIES, UNITE!" Those later writers who have wondered why Marx and Engels would exhort the workers to revolt against the exploiters in a rising that they treat as absolutely inevitable simply fail to comprehend the minds of Marx and Engels as men who were not only thinkers but would-be leaders of a movement. As such they found it natural to couple their definition of the proletarians' situation with a prescription of what should be done.

The community whose situation the *Manifesto* seeks to define is not a nation-state—as with much conventional constituted political leadership—but a social class. This class it views as universal, as mankind itself *in statu nascendi*, on the ground that masses of people in all modern bourgeois societies are being proletarianized and that all nonbourgeois societies are becoming, or are fated to become, bourgeois. What the *Manifesto* purports to diagnose is thus the human situation, and this in the context of all past history as a progression of humanity through one form of class-divided society to another, each time via a social revolution that marks the ascendancy of a new mode of productive labor. Capitalist wage labor figures in this sequence as the last exploitative mode prior to the last revolution, which by socializing the means of production will create a classless, stateless, worldwide community of man where human productive activity will not be exploited for gain.

Such is the *Manifesto*'s vision of a radically new society, a community of producers, whose basic culture pattern, real and ideal alike, will be free creativity of associated human beings producing according to their abilities and receiving according to their needs. As revolutionaries, Marx and Engels pour scorn on the ideal culture patterns of the society they would abolish—upon "bourgeois notions of freedom, culture, law, etc.," upon "bourgeois individuality, bourgeois independence, and bourgeois freedom." They deride that society's libertarian sustaining myth as its "religious and political illusions," as ideological sham and hypocrisy. They criticize socialist reformers, like the Owenites in England, who wished to attain communitarian ends by peaceful means of persuasion, as obstructors of revolutionary class war.[20] And in a passage elsewhere that conveys the essence of the reform mentality with total clarity by polemizing against it from a revolutionary's point of view, Marx decries the reformist socialism that "only idealizes society, takes a picture of it without shadows and wants to achieve its ideal athwart the realities of present society."[21]

The initiatives by which founding leaders help bring movements into being by their persuasive new ways of diagnosing collective situations and prescribing courses of action in them naturally do not exhaust the range of movement leadership, whether for reform or for revolution. Once movements arise and become organized, with

20. The citations from the *Manifesto* in this and the previous paragraph appear in *The Marx-Engels Reader*, ed. Robert C. Tucker, 2d ed. (New York: W. W. Norton, 1978), pp. 475, 485, 487, 499, and 500.
21. *The Class Struggles in France*, in ibid., p. 592.

ideologies and established patterns of political action to promote their ends, the movement leaders, like any other, must go on functioning as leaders in changing constellations of circumstances by further diagnosing problem situations and further prescribing responses to those situations. Grand diagnoses that take all human history as their context, such as Marx's, are no more than momentous starting points in movement leadership, even for Marxist movements. Sometimes movement leadership consists in a revisionist redefining of the collective situation by leaders who, like Eduard Bernstein in the German Social Democratic movement of the end of the nineteenth century, find meanings in new sets of circumstances that indicate, at least to them, the need for new ways of thought and action by the movement. What started as a movement for revolution can in this manner undergo transformation into a movement for reform.

It can happen, alternatively, that a mind of uncompromisingly revolutionary orientation will diagnose circumstances themselves as the problem and prescribe action to change the circumstances in the interest of realizing the movement's original revolutionary goals. In such a case, the needs of the movement as a revolutionary one have been uppermost in the leader's mind in his definition of what the circumstances mean. A historic exemplar is Lenin in his seminal pamphlet of 1902, *What Is To Be Done?*, which can be seen as the key act of leadership that brought Russian Communism into being as, initially, a current within the larger, already existing Russian Marxist movement.

Here Lenin took as his starting point the threat that "Economism," a Russian Marxist counterpart to Bernsteinian revisionism in Germany, presented to Russian Marxist revolutionism. The underlying source of the danger, according to the pamphlet's way of diagnosing the situation of the working-class movement around the turn of the century, was the workers' spontaneous tendency toward "trade-union consciousness," meaning an orientation on improving workers' conditions economically, ignoring the need for revolutionary overthrow of the capitalist system. This was implicitly a definition of the situation deviant from Marx's position that capitalist conditions themselves must revolutionize the workers.

From it Lenin drew the conclusion, as a policy response, that the need of the movement was to "combat spontaneity" through revolutionary propaganda and agitation, which in Russia's police-state conditions would have to be conducted clandestinely by small groups of professional revolutionaries acting as missionaries of revolutionary consciousness among all groups of the czar's subjects with grievances against the existing regime; and that this required, as a prime condition of success, the creation of a small, close-knit, conspiratorially organized political party capable of acting as the conscious vanguard of large masses of the people in their movement toward an ultimate revolutionary settling of accounts with czarism. Here, in embryo, was not only a neo-Marxist definition of the collective situation but also a new prescription for action that contained within itself, no doubt without Lenin's being aware of it at the time, a kind of prospectus for the one-party system and the sustaining myth of the new Soviet Russian society that was going to arise on the yonder side of the taking of power by Lenin's party in October 1917.

That turning point in history was itself a consequence, in part, of Lenin's creative situation-defining activity in movement politics. Russia's February Revolution in 1917 swept away czarist rule and created a democratic provisional government in which the Bolsheviks did not participate. In the early aftermath, while Lenin remained in Switzerland, Bolshevik leaders in Petrograd, including Stalin, did not diagnose the new set of circumstances prevailing in the country as revolutionary. Their minds were in the grip of a stereotype or type-situation according to which a "bourgeois-democratic" revolution like Russia's February one must be separated by a considerable time interval from a socialist one. So, as they saw it in March 1917, the situation was for the time being postrevolutionary, and Bolshevism's proper policy response was to exert all possible pressure upon the provisional government to take Russia out of the World War.

Lenin, however, still in Swiss exile, was of a different mind. In an article of 1915, as if anticipating the present occasion, he had set forth a general conception of what constitutes a "revolutionary situation." There are, he said, three main symptoms: a crisis "up above," in the policy of the ruling class; an unusual aggravation of the privation and tribulations of the oppressed classes; and a substantial rise, for these reasons, in the level of mass activity.[22] Now, from afar, he interpreted the circumstances of free, war-weary, and incipiently turbulent Russian society in those terms. Immediately upon arriving in Petrograd in early April, he issued a set of "theses" on party policy that were in contradiction with the party leadership's definition of the situation hitherto in force. The "theses" diagnosed Russia's situation as revolutionary and on that basis prescribed for the Bolshevik movement a revolution-oriented policy of opposition to the provisional government under the slogan, All Power to the Soviets![23] By dint of hard persuasion, Lenin overcame the initial reluctance of various other leading Bolsheviks to view the

22. Lenin, "The Symptoms of a Revolutionary Situation," in *The Lenin Anthology*, ed. Robert C. Tucker (New York: W. W. Norton, 1975), p. 275.

23. For Lenin's "April Theses," see ibid., pp. 295–300.

situation in that light and rallied the party's support for his position.

Here we see how an act of leadership can be self-fulfilling: it can help bring about the very situation that the leader has diagnosed as already existing. The militant new political stance that the Bolshevik party adopted under Lenin's influence proved to be one of the factors that converted the latently revolutionary situation of Russian society into the actually revolutionary one that obtained in the autumn when, following Lenin's urgings, the party launched the successful coup by which it took power. Leadership in this case decisively contributed to one of history's mighty lurches.

If Lenin was, as Hook argued, an "event-making" rather than a merely "eventful" man in 1917, that is because of the effective way in which he performed the functions of a leader in the politics of the Bolshevik revolutionary movement.

4

Leadership and the Human Situation

Political leadership's basic tasks, we have argued, are to define the collective situation, to design ways of dealing with it, and to mobilize support for the diagnosis and proposed mode of response. These things can be done, or at least attempted, by nonconstituted as well as constituted leaders. As it happens, nonconstituted leaders are mainly the ones who have sought to diagnose and devise courses of action in the situation about to be discussed. Briefly, man has become an endangered species. A crisis of human survival is emerging.

This diagnosis is a departure from normal political thinking in its conception of the composition of the political community. According to conventional thought, it is nation-states, or parts of them, or groupings of them, that confront problem situations in which action is needed. For the view here taken, the group *in* the situation is, in fact, all the people, the entire population of what has come to be called "spaceship earth." Let us note that "all the people" now comprise well over 4 billion souls. The estimated world population in 1975 was 4.1 billion.

Recognition that a crisis of human survival is emerging has spread among practical people as well as among professional intellectuals. The former include several members of the commission set up by the president of the World Bank, Robert McNamara, to conduct, under the chairmanship of former West German Chancellor Willy Brandt, an inquiry into world trends from the standpoint of North–South relations. Earlier contributions came from the Club of Rome, an informal organization originally comprising thirty persons from ten countries who gathered in Rome in 1968 to consider the human prospect. Later, it grew to about seventy persons of twenty-five nationalities, none holding public office and representing no particular ideology or national point of view. It began a "Project on the Predicament of Mankind" whose first report, issued in 1972, was called *The Limits to Growth*, and whose second, published in 1974, was called *Mankind at the Turning Point*. Now, for the first time, the resources of a major government, that of the United States, have been mobilized to make a projection of world developments to the end of the twentieth century. The resulting *Global 2000* report, prepared by the Council on Environmental Quality and the Department of State on the basis of information provided by thirteen agencies of the federal government, was published in 1980 in three volumes.

My first purpose here is to present a short distillation of some trends of thinking reflected in such documents, in order then to consider their implications from a leadership perspective. Their conclusions, however cautiously worded, support the definition of man's situation as an emerging crisis of survival. The Brandt commission's report says that "immense risks are threatening mankind" and that "prospects for the future are alarming. At the beginning of the 1980's the world community faces much greater dangers than at any time since the Second World War."[1] In more restrained language, perhaps because of

1. *North-South: A Programme for Survival: Report of the Independent Commission on International Development Issues* (Cambridge, Mass.: MIT Press, 1980), pp. 25, 267.

its governmental auspices, *Global 2000* states, "If present trends continue, the world in 2000 will be more crowded, more polluted, less stable ecologically, and more vulnerable to disruption than the world we live in now."[2]

The Crisis Syndrome

What is the problem and why is it so serious? It appears to lie in the interplay of a whole series of problems advancing upon us at frightening speed. To cite *Mankind at the Turning Point*, while arms reduction is a prerequisite for lasting peace,

> there is a much more subtle and completely novel threat to man's survival that looms, every year more menacingly, beside that of an atomic holocaust: the cluster of worldwide problems—not only material in nature—growing at an incredible speed when viewed in historical perspective, and called by The Club of Rome the "*problématique humaine.*" In fact, we believe that even without an atomic world war, human existence as we know it is threatened if no way can be found to resolve this crisis syndrome.[3]

To explicate the "crisis syndrome," even summarily, is more than my space and competence permit. I will attempt the lesser task of indicating some of its elements and their interrelations.

A principal element is the steadily continuing population growth on a planet with finite limits and resources. According to *North-South*, over 1 million people are added every five days to the 4-billion-plus passengers on

2. *The Global 2000 Report to the President: Entering the Twenty-First Century* (Washington, D.C.: U.S. Government Printing Office, 1980), 1: 1.

3. Mihajlo Mesarovic and Eduard Pestel, *Mankind at the Turning Point: The Second Report to The Club of Rome* (New York: E. P. Dutton, 1974), p. xi.

spaceship earth. That refers to net growth, the excess of births over deaths.[4] In some countries the population is now stationary, in some the growth is very slow. In many others, however, and they are the poorest, the growth rate is still large, and even if the overall growth *rate* has leveled off, as demographers report, growth itself, they admit, will continue. By 2000, according to *Global 2000*, the world's population will be 6.35 billion, or 50 percent more than in 1975, and will be growing by 100 million a year, a growth rate that, if continued, would result in a world population of 10 billion by 2030 and something approaching 30 billion by 2100.[5] To grasp the possible implications of these figures, we should reflect that, according to some estimates, about 1 billion out of the present 4 are either starving or going hungry. These people live and die chiefly in the Third World. The United Nations Children's Fund has estimated that more than 12 million children under the age of five died of hunger in 1978 alone.[6] If one out of four of us is starving or going hungry now, what will it be like when we are six or eight instead of four?

This question brings us to a second widely recognized element of the crisis syndrome: the depletion of resources. Because the fuel-energy dimension of this is so familiar, I will dwell instead on food resources. The central fact is that, despite a projected increase of world food production by an annual 2.2 percent between 1970 and 2000, which would outstrip the aggregate projected population growth, the outlook is not promising. First, increases in food production are being achieved by means

4. *North-South*, p. 105.
5. *Global 2000*, pp. 1, 3. *North-South* states that nine-tenths of the two-billion increase by 2000 will take place in the Third World (p. 105).
6. *North-South*, p. 16.

that in the end will reduce the possibilities of food production. A key fact is soil erosion owing to the loss of fertile topsoil, necessary for agriculture, at rates that greatly exceed the natural rates of replacement. There is worldwide loss of topsoil through overcropping and planting on hillsides. In the United States, despite the existence of soil conservation programs, erosion is proceeding at an alarming rate, largely because, in a rural economy affected by such phenomena as steeply increased land value, absentee ownership of farmlands, and high demand by foreign buyers, farmers are bringing into cultivation more and more marginal land, reducing the cycles of rotation, and more and more planting such high-return crops as corn and soybeans at the expense of the grass and clover that restore soil. One writer notes that if these trends continue, the United States will lose its food-exporting capacity.[7] "We are on a collision course with disaster," said former U.S. Secretary of Agriculture Bob Bergland. "Water supplies are being reduced, and the erosion of American farmland today is probably at a record high. This simply cannot go on."[8]

To soil erosion must be added desertification as a force for eventual decline of food production. In North Africa, for example, much arable land is lost annually to the encroaching Sahara Desert. Desertification takes place in some western parts of the United States too. Urbanization consumes much cropland. In the United States an estimated 2 million acres of cropland are lost every year to highways, urbanization, and other special uses. In France, the equivalent of one of its eighty-three *départ-*

7. Ann Crittenden, "Soil Erosion Threatens U.S. Farms' Output," *The New York Times*, 26 October 1980. The cited source for the estimate that by 2000 the United States will have to stop exporting food in order to feed itself is Ned Bayley, Assistant Secretary of Agriculture for Conservation, Resources, and Environment.

8. *The New York Times*, 27 November 1978.

ments disappears under concrete every five years. Irrigation, in the absence of expensive drainage systems, damages much land owing to salinity.

Many of the world's forest resources, on which much of mankind depends for cooking and heating, are shrinking owing to transformation into farmland or simply to the fact that they are consumed at a rate in excess of natural replacement. A tropical forest area the size of Delaware, it is estimated, goes into development every week, and population increase is putting huge pressure on jungle ecosystems.[9] An ecological authority, Eric Eckholm, points out that loss of forestlands accelerates erosion of croplands and siltation of streams and rivers, causing deserts to grow and flooding problems to worsen, and he estimates that in Africa, Asia, and Latin America forest areas are declining annually by an area the size of Cuba.[10] *Global 2000* finds that food from fish will not meet the needs of the swiftly rising global population because the world fish harvest will hardly increase by 2000 and pressure on water resources will grow due to increasing demand by more and more people for fresh water. Already serious, regional water shortages and deterioration of water quality are likely to get worse by 2000.[11]

Now we can formulate more fully the Club of Rome's concept of a crisis "syndrome" involving the interplay of several crises that aggravate one another. Ever growing population exerts ever increasing pressure on resources, many of which have become, or at some point will become, diminishing ones. Developmental efforts to meet

9. Edward S. Ayensu, "In the Jungle, We Know Not What We Do," *The New York Times*, 19 July 1980. Mr. Ayensu is director of the Smithsonian Institution's Office of Biological Conservation.

10. *The New York Times*, 18 February 1979.

11. *Global 2000*, pp. 21, 26.

119

heightened world demand can often do so only at the expense of future man's resource needs. Population growth and some modes of utilizing eventually diminishing resources aggravate a third major crisis in the syndrome—environmental degradation. We are polluting our planet as we grow in numbers, as technologies advance, as many of our cities turn into interminable urban sprawls, and as we exploit our resources to meet insatiable demand. Thus, mankind's use of the seas and some of the great lakes, such as America's Lake Erie and Russia's Lake Baikal, as dumping grounds for industrial wastes harmful to marine ecosystems has threatened the biological future of those bodies of water. This danger is magnified by oil spills caused by tanker mishaps and oil-well drilling blowouts.

Earlier we took note of Rachel Carson's diagnosis of the danger that widespread use of chemical pesticides poses to wildlife. Her concluding chapter opened with characteristic leadership language:

> We stand now where two roads diverge. But unlike the roads of Robert Frost's familiar poem, they are not equally fair. The road we have long been traveling is deceptively easy, a smooth, superhighway on which we progress with great speed, but at its end lies disaster. The other fork of the road—the one "less traveled by"—offers our last, our only chance to reach a destination that assures the preservation of our earth.[12]

By the "other fork" she meant the use of biological solutions as alternatives to the chemical control of insects. That was 1962. Whatever the importance of *Silent Spring* in stimulating an ecological movement, America, nearly two decades later, has not taken the other fork or swerved

12. Rachel Carson, *Silent Spring* (New York: Fawcett, 1962), p. 244.

far from the smooth superhighway. It is still confronted
with problems caused by pesticides. Although corrective
action has been taken in the form of enactment of federal
laws banning domestic use of pesticides known to have
harmful effects, the law permits their export as well as the
export of others that have not yet been evaluated and ap-
proved for U.S. use. It is reported that huge quantities of
such substances are exported to third-world countries
where they are used in the growing of foods that are exported to, among other places, the United States and consumed in products bought in our supermarkets. "In a
world of growing food interdependence," says the report,
"we cannot export our hazards and then forget them.
There is no refuge. The mushrooming use of pesticides in
the Third World is a daily threat to millions there—and a
growing threat to all consumers here."[13]

Food interdependence is accompanied by other
forms of the same phenomenon, including air interdependence. Nations that follow the earlier precedents set by
the United States and Soviet Russia of testing nuclear
weapons atmospherically, and those that may do so in
future if further proliferation of nuclear weapons takes
place, release radioactive fallout into air that travels
around the globe. Again, as it became clear that chemicals called chlorofluorocarbons released by aerosol sprays
may dangerously deplete the stratospheric ozone layer,
which protects life on earth from too much ultraviolet radiation, U.S. federal regulators banned the use of most
aerosol sprays. Yet the danger goes on rising because
chlorofluorocarbons are in increasing industrial use in

13. David Weir and Mark Schapiro, "The Circle of Poisons," *The
Nation*, 15 November 1980. The authors of this article, which sum-
marizes a forthcoming book, are staff members of the Center for Inves-
tigative Reporting in Oakland, California.

America, and their use, partly in spray cans, is growing abroad.[14] Truly, there is no refuge.

A further form of environmental degradation, ground and water pollution caused by toxic-waste dumps and chemical spills, was dramatized by the disaster in the Love Canal area of Niagara Falls, New York, many of whose residents had to be evacuated from their homes owing to birth defects, miscarriages, and increased cancer rates resulting from exposure to toxic chemicals. A journalist, Michael Brown, has acted as a nonconstituted leader by defining this danger situation in its full national dimensions. His research has shown that such time bombs are now strewn across America, where about one thousand new chemicals are added yearly to the seventy thousand that already exist. Information obtained from the U.S. Environmental Protection Agency (EPA) indicated that by 1979 there were over 32,000 *known* sites where hazardous wastes were stored or buried and that 838 of these were potentially "significant imminent hazards" to public health. The word *known* is emphasized because great amounts of toxic wastes have been dumped in unknown sites. In the later 1970s, approximately 35 million tons of hazardous wastes were being generated each year, compared with 10 million tons in 1970. The EPA estimated that under 70 percent of the wastes received proper disposal. Brown concludes his book with poignant leadership language. The epilogue—on possible ways of halting and undoing the contamination of our land—is entitled "The Road Back."[15]

If the manifold processes comprised in the crisis syn-

14. "The Dilemma of the Endangered Ozone," *The New York Times*, 29 October 1980.

15. Michael H. Brown, *Laying Waste: The Poisoning of America By Toxic Chemicals* (New York: Pantheon Books, 1980), pp. 289, 293–94, 325–35.

drome continue unchecked and civilization is not meanwhile destroyed by nuclear war, then somewhere down
the line, seventy-five or a hundred years hence if not
sooner, our problem-wracked world of 1980 will seem a
golden twilight of evanescent normalcy, and people will
look back in wonder or in anger at those now alive who
could comprehend what lay ahead and might have tried
by resolute concerted action to avert the descent into disaster, yet did not. Unless, that is, political leadership
effectively intervenes to change the prospect.

Leadership as Antileadership

So far there is no sign of that happening. While time
is running out for humanity, the governments of the approximately one hundred and fifty nation-states now in
existence try to do political business as usual. Constituted
leaders show little tendency toward forms of thinking and
acting anew that would meet the challenge of a "case" so
radically new. Let us take, for example, a recent statement
of outlook by a former British prime minister, Edward
Heath, a man with thirty years' experience of political life
and the larger latitude for thinking anew that is characteristic of one no longer in political office. He begins
promisingly: "There comes a point in every crisis when
the political leaders should disengage from the immediate
operations, stand back and assess the whole situation
afresh." What is his fresh assessment? The Soviet Union,
he says, has a world strategy for maintaining and furthering its interests whereas the West has no such strategy, but
badly needs one as a counterpoint to Russia's. In the remainder of the statement,[16] Mr. Heath presents his view of
what such a counterstrategy should be, showing no

16. *The New York Times*, 19 March 1980.

awareness that the issues in East–West relations, serious though they be, call for consideration in the context of the oncoming crisis of survival.

Political business as usual basically continues to prevail in both the internal lives and external relations of nation-states. Military expenditures absorb an estimated 6 percent of the world's gross national product, 25 percent of its scientific talent, and 40 percent of its efforts in research and development.[17] Small wars between states in the Third World are increasing in numbers, while chaos, disorder, and turmoil spread in that whole vast region of the globe.[18] Meanwhile, the superpowers continue or intensify their contest for political influence over various countries of the Third World, with the above-mentioned periodic destabilizing effects on their efforts to cooperate in certain areas such as arms control. All this belongs to the *problématique*. National governments' persistent pursuit of normal politics in the present era must be considered a key element of the crisis situation.

This judgment needs some qualifying. The governments, or some of them, have not been altogether insensitive to problems touched upon here, and efforts toward their solution or control have not been wholly lacking. Japan, with its heavily peopled island territory, and more recently China, which accounts for about a quarter of mankind, have adopted strong policies of birth control. The Scandinavian states have cooperated in taking steps to check the polluting of their shared Baltic Sea. Amer-

17. Ruth L. Sivard, "Let Them Eat Bullets," *Bulletin of the Atomic Scientists* 31: 4 (1975): 9.

18. See the survey of the situation by Fouad Ajami in "The Fate of Nonalignment," *Foreign Affairs* (Winter 1980). On the rising numbers of small wars in the Third World, now running at the rate of 1.6 a year according to political scientist Lincoln P. Bloomfield, see Tad Szulc, "The Refugee Explosion," *The New York Times Magazine*, 23 November 1980, p. 138.

ica's EPA has fought, often without success because of industry's opposition, against the continuing pollution of our land by chemical toxicants. Congress has furnished leadership, albeit belatedly, by enacting a Resources Conservation and Recovery Act to ensure in future the safe management of hazardous chemicals and other wastes. In the 1970s the United Nations sponsored a series of world conferences on the environment, population, food, and the law of the sea, but they accomplished little more than establishment of a United Nations Environment Program for monitoring and coordinating purposes and still uncompleted negotiation of a treaty on the law of the sea. In general, these and other small beginnings are dwarfed by the scale of the problems addressed.

The leaders of national governments are in default by failing to fulfill the first function of political leadership—the authoritative defining of the situation for the political community. If they are aware that time is running out for man, they are keeping silent about it in communicating with their peoples. It is indicative that *Global 2000*, perhaps a first major move toward such official communicating, was issued not as a report endorsed *by* the president of the United States but as one *to* him, and in the subsequent national election campaign of 1980 neither of the two main contenders seems to have discussed its contents and implications publicly.

Default of leadership by constituted authority, failure to diagnose collectively meaningful circumstances as problem situations calling for action, has been discussed earlier in these pages. But how shall we account for nondefinition in this unprecedented instance, when developing circumstances place man's long-term survival in question? One part of the answer lies in the limited time-horizon of the conventional leadership culture as formed in the past and still operative. We have seen that problem situations can have a future dimension, a foreseeable tendency to develop further in a particular direction, especially if nothing is done to counteract that. This emphatically applies to the emerging planetary situation. Its manifestations so far experienced—such as mass starvation and malnutrition in some parts of the world, difficulties arising from incipient depletion of resources and rising pollution, the spread of huge numbers of refugees beyond national boundaries owing to local wars, famine, unemployment, and the brutality of dictatorial regimes—are, for all their gravity, no more than advance indications of far worse yet to come. But conventional political leadership is not minded to define the situation in its future dimensions. It is oriented to the political here and now. A political scientist has aptly characterized this attitude as one of "adhocracy" or "muddling through," meaning that "it focuses on the problem immediately at hand and tries to find the solution that is most congruent with the status quo."[19]

In the case before us, the "problem immediately at hand" is one or another symptom of an infinitely deeper and more complex crisis syndrome that will generate increasingly serious, increasingly intractable problems at hand with each passing decade. Constituted political leaders, however, do not normally think and act in terms of how situations will predictably develop two or three decades hence. The usual horizon of concern is the coming few years of a leader's or a party's anticipated time in political office. Liberal democracies with multiparty systems may be especially vulnerable to this obstacle to effective leadership because, apart from the time-horizon factor just mentioned, forthright public diagnosis of the

19. William Ophuls, *Ecology and the Politics of Scarcity: Prologue to a Political Theory of the Steady State* (San Francisco: W. H. Freeman, 1977), pp. 191, 193.

evolving planetary situation, implying as it might the need for a new popular ethos consonant with a coming age of scarcity, could assure one's rival's victory in an election.[20]

History has shown that democratically governed societies are capable of responding positively to leadership's call for sacrifice and self-denial when confronted with the dramatically visible crisis situation that war can create. But the emerging crisis of survival, owing to its long-term character, its immense complexity, and its uneven impact upon regions and peoples at the present stage, is not dramatically visible in still well-off parts of the world. It is an insidious crisis, and for that reason all the harder for even an enlightened leadership, if such existed, to diagnose in a politically persuasive enough way for effective mobilizing of response. If in spite of everything that were to happen, however, the response would be that of the political community of a nation-state and hence necessarily of limited effect.

Because the crisis situation is global in scope and eventual impact, it demands a globally concerted set of actions to bring the syndrome under control. But there exists, as yet, no "central guidance capability"[21] to furnish planetary political leadership of an authoritative kind. Here again the problem is rooted in normal leadership culture and the normal nation-state political cultures in which leaders function. It is generally accepted that the proper purpose of a nation-state's political leadership is to foster the good of the national political community, to serve the "national interest." An aspiring political leader

20. "It is hardly to be expected that our elected officials will commit political suicide by forcing unpopular environmental measures on us," writes Ophuls, adding, "one way or another, we Americans are about to find out what kind of people we are" (ibid., pp. 197, 198).

21. The concept is Richard A. Falk's. See his *A Study of Future Worlds* (New York: The Free Press, 1975), pp. 156–58, 234.

has to avow a supreme allegiance to the nation's interest as the price of acquiring the desired leadership role; and an incumbent leader has to do the same as the price of preserving it. To become a constituted political leader in the modern world is virtually to enter a compact with the political community to promote its interests in all ways at all times.

Such being the case, the prospect is more ominous than might be suggested by my use of the phrase *default of leadership* in commenting on constituted authority's failure to apprise the peoples of the emerging crisis of survival. It is more ominous because political leadership of some sort *is and will be forthcoming* as syndrome-linked circumstances confront nation-states in ways that impel their leaders to diagnose problem situations in national terms and devise responses in short-term national interests. This will intensify international conflict—on a globe where nuclear-weapon technology shows signs of proliferating beyond all control. The Club of Rome's computerized projections have led it to forecast a "tug of war for scarce resources" and therewith an intensification of conflict and confrontation in the "new age of scarcity" that is coming or already upon us, although its preferred future is a combination of conservation and cooperation.[22] With respect to the likelihood of intensified international conflict for dwindling resources, the Club of Rome's view is no different from that of so representative a man of normal leadership culture as Henry Kissinger, who in an interview in 1974 foresaw the possibility that Western civilization will disintegrate because of:

> a series of rivalries in which each region will try to maximize its own special advantages. That, inevitably, will lead

22. Mesarovic and Pestel, *Mankind at the Turning Point*, chaps. 7 and 8. See also Ophuls, *Ecology and the Politics of Scarcity*, p. 214.

to tests of strength. . . . These will magnify domestic crises in many countries, and they will then move more and more to authoritarian models. I would expect then that we will certainly have crises which no leadership is able to deal with, and probably military confrontations.[23]

Following the pathways of normal leadership culture, the governments of major "have" countries or areas, especially those with great power, will probably pursue courses of action designed to shore up their own political community's relatively favored position and continued habitual existence while the less favored and less powerful sink deeper and deeper into a morass of hopeless chaos and misery. In such a world of *sauve qui peut*, a political community's salvation will be at best a protracted temporary mirage and events will finally get out of control. Here we reach the paradox of leadership as anti-leadership, meaning that constituted political leadership, precisely when most effective in furthering the short-term parochial interest of one section of humanity, will work against the requirements of leadership in the interest of all, one of which is global peace during what could be an era of transition to a workable way of life for the species.

All of which suggests still another definition of the emerging crisis. So far in history, people have looked for political leadership to one or another territorial state formation ranging from the city-states of classical antiquity to the great nation-states of modern times. Always the assumption has been that governments of the various politically organized portions of the globe could, in principle, take care of the leadership needs of the human groups in which they have exercised authority. This assumption has lost validity. The capacity of human civilization to endure on earth has come to depend upon the development of

23. *The New York Times*, 12 October 1974.

leadership *of and for the whole*. The emerging crisis of survival is, along with all else, one of leadership deficiency. The spaceship cannot fly much longer unpiloted.

The Party of Humanity

When constituted leadership is in default, we have seen, it often happens that nonconstituted leadership arises, seeking to define the collective situation and to devise desirable courses of action for meeting it. Such nonconstituted leaders may also try to mobilize support for their view of what the situation is and what should be done about it. If they succeed, a movement arises. Applying these generalities to the case at hand, let us now see how nonconstituted leaders have in fact come forward and consider some of their thinking and its effects.

Universalistic thinking about man and his earthly future developed among the philosophes of the eighteenth-century Enlightenment, a group called by one of our contemporary historians the "party of humanity."[24] I propose to bestow this title upon a scattered company of twentieth-century people who have acted as nonconstituted leaders of a still nonexistent community of man by diagnosing the crisis of survival from a global perspective and envisioning ways of overcoming it. One could start the story with the correspondence of the 1930s in which Albert Einstein and Sigmund Freud agreed that humanity was in danger of self-destruction through further great wars like that of 1914–1918.[25] For our purposes, however, it will be convenient to consider some trends of thought in the later decades of the twentieth century, when the con-

24. Peter Gay, *The Party of Humanity: Essays in the French Enlightenment* (Princeton: Princeton University Press, 1959).
25. For Freud's position, see "Why War?," in Sigmund Freud, *Character and Culture* (New York: Collier Books, 1963), pp. 134–47.

tours of crisis have become increasingly visible. Since the *problématique* has already been discussed in some salient aspects, we shall give special attention to what has been proposed by way of response.

The party of humanity is notably diverse in nationality and profession. People from very many lands have become members by the mental act of joining and then by participating, so far mainly as thinkers, in the leadership activity itself. Alongside economists like Kenneth Boulding and Barbara Ward, we find writers like Isaac Bashevis Singer, psychologists like Erik H. Erikson, legal scholars like Lewis Sohn and Grenville Clark, the associates of their recently founded World Order Models Project, and even a onetime constituted leader like Willy Brandt. There are clergymen, industrialists, and civil servants. Some members are among the famous names of the twentieth century, such as the late German doctor and philosopher, Albert Schweitzer; the late Frenchman known as the architect of Europe, Jean Monnet; the late Mohandas Gandhi and his late American disciple, Martin Luther King; and the late Dag Hammarskjöld, who was secretary general of the United Nations. The party of humanity is so numerous and full of talent that anyone's list of outstanding members must be, like mine, very much a personal document.

The party is not political in the ordinary sense; it is not a power-seeking group but a leadership cohort. It could be described as a moral party with a shared ethic that Schweitzer called "reverence for life." Its members also share a refusal to despair in face of a human predicament that they have diagnosed in various ways as grim and getting grimmer. Their refusal to give way to hopelessness rests upon a faith in man's capacity to choose the path ahead and be guided by reason, foresight, and goodwill in doing so. Some have made statements that sound

131

pessimistic, as Schweitzer did when he said, "Man has lost the capacity to foresee and to forestall. He will end by destroying the earth." But I doubt that Carson would have chosen that line as the epigraph to *Silent Spring* if she had not thought it inspired by a passion to falsify its prophecy.

The party of humanity's "No!" to hopelessness has not been better put than by Isaac Bashevis Singer, when he spoke in the Swedish Academy in 1978 upon receiving the Nobel Prize for literature, in this instance literature in Yiddish: "As the son of a people who received the worst blows that human madness can inflict, I must brood about the forthcoming dangers. I have many times resigned myself to never finding a true way out. But a new hope always emerges telling me it is not yet too late for all of us to take stock and make a decision." Jean Monnet, in memoirs published as he approached the age of ninety, expressed it in his Gallic way:

> I am not an optimist. I am simply persistent. If action is necessary, how can one say that it is impossible, so long as one has not tried it? . . . There can be no progress without a certain disorder on the surface. . . . The problem is to organize change. . . . Events that strike me and occupy my thoughts lead me to general conclusions about what has to be done. . . . I can wait a long time for the right moment. In Cognac, they are good at waiting. It is the only way to make good brandy.[26]

The party of humanity's leadership activity consists not only in diagnosing the crisis situation but also in seeking, through wide dissemination and persuasive analysis of the evidence for the diagnosis, to mobilize support by making people at large aware of the true nature of man's present and prospective situation. Kenneth Boulding has conveyed this pedagogical dimension of the leadership

26. Jean Monnet, *Mémoires* (Paris: Fayard, 1976), p. 44.

activity by picturing the party as an "invisible college" of people of diverse countries, cultures, religions, philosophies, and political positions who share the vision of a world in transition and the will to do all they can to assist the transition to occur. He goes on:

> It is a college without a founder and without a president, without buildings and without organization. Its founding members might have included a Jesuit like Pierre Teilhard de Chardin, a humanist like Aldous Huxley, a writer of science fiction like H. G. Wells, and it might even have given honorary degrees to Adam Smith, Karl Marx, Pope John XXIII, and even to Khrushchev and John F. Kennedy. Its living representatives are still a pretty small group of people. I think, however, that it is they who hold the future of the world in their hands or at least in their minds.[27]

To join the invisible college of transition implies, he writes, a change from the unexamined to the examined life, a change that flows first from the realization that "this blue-green cradle of life" is in a position of immense danger and immense potentiality, and then from the commitment to make a constructive contribution along whatever are the lines of one's abilities. Another member of the party, or the invisible college, speaks of the need to work toward producing a "change of consciousness" or "metanoia" that will permit people "to see a new kind of reality based on ecological understanding."[28]

The party of humanity's leadership activity has been heavily concerned with the devising of possible courses of

27. Kenneth E. Boulding, *The Meaning of the Twentieth Century: The Great Transition* (New York: Harper & Row, 1964), pp. 191–92.
28. Ophuls, *Ecology and the Politics of Scarcity*, p. 223. See also Falk, *Future Worlds*, p. 290, where he writes: "One of the tasks of a world order movement is to provide people everywhere with better tools to understand both the costs and dangers of the present world order system, and the realistic prospects for its decisive improvement."

action in the crisis situation. A considerable consensus prevails in the now large body of literature pertaining to desirable ecological forms of response. The underlying leitmotiv is that man must place his planetary existence on an equilibrium, bringing levels of consumption and modes of living into balance with the potentialities of the environment, the finiteness of some resources and the re-newability of others, the preservation of our natural sur-roundings, and the needs of equity. The first report to the Club of Rome broached the idea of an end to growth. The second modified this by distinguishing between desirable forms of "organic growth" involving, for example, the re-dressing of a regional imbalance in food production, and the still continuing "unbalanced and undifferentiated growth" that leads to ultimate disaster. It calls for an atti-tude toward nature "based on harmony rather than con-quest" and a "new ethic in the use of material resources . . . which will result in a style of life compatible with the oncoming age of scarcity."[29] Another formulation refers to the need to create, on a planetary basis, a "steady-state society" characterized by "primary dependence on income or flow resources, the maintenance of population levels within the ecological carrying capacity, resources conser-vation and recycling, generally good ecological husband-ry." The writer adds that ecology thus conceived is "a fun-damentally conservative orientation to the world."[30]

The ecological response will require, our leadership cohort stresses, attitudinal change among people at large. It thus necessitates an educational or consciousness-changing effort that goes far beyond the fostering of clearer intellectual understanding of the emerging situa-tion. The reference in the Club of Rome's second report to

29. Mesarovic and Pestel, *Mankind at the Turning Point*, pp. 3–9, 147.
30. Ophuls, *Ecology and the Politics of Scarcity*, pp. 226, 234.

a new ethic in the use of material resources and a new attitude toward nature is indicative of what is envisaged. William Ophuls predicates a politics of the steady state upon a "move away from the values of growth, profligacy, and exploitation typical of 'economic man' toward sufficiency, frugality, and stewardship"; this last value, he goes on, will become the cardinal virtue of ecological economics.[31]

Along with the ecological theme, the political and organizational one has a major place in the party of humanity's thinking about modes of response. These are not denationalized people. Monnet, to take one example, was a quintessential Frenchman. Yet I think he spoke for most of our leadership cohort when he wrote in his memoirs: "The sovereign nations of the past can no longer solve the problems of the present [in this one hears an echo, unconscious no doubt, of "The dogmas of the quiet past are inadequate to the stormy present"]. They cannot ensure their own progress or control their own future. And the European community itself is only a stage on the way to the organized world of tomorrow."[32]

What forms the "organized world of tomorrow" might feasibly take, by what stages it might be brought into being, and what means might be most efficacious in building it peacefully, are questions to which some powerful minds have been devoting much time and thought. Results range from the straightforward plan for world government set forth in Clark and Sohn's *World Peace through World Law* (1960) to the more modulated, long-range, political- as well as legal-minded plan for transformative structural change devised by the American group in the World Order Models Project. The plan em-

31. Ibid., p. 229. Perhaps on this account, he also suggests that "Metanoia is tantamount to religious conversion" (p. 243).

32. Monnet, *Mémoires*, p. 617.

phasizes the function of "central guidance," envisaging the step-by-step emergence of such guidance structures as a world polity association, a council of principals, a central coordinating board, world security forces, and a world grievance system. In designing this world-order system, the authors of the plan have made a commitment to "minimizing the degree of bureaucratic and coercive centralism."[33]

According to the analysis presented in the preceding chapter, social movements often arise when there is widespread distress or a sense of the need for change, when constituted authority fails to diagnose the circumstances involved as a problem situation calling for collective action toward change, and when nonconstituted leaders come forward with such diagnoses and with proposals for courses of action aimed at bringing about change. To a great extent these conditions are met in the present context. Yet no movement of major significance has emerged in response to our leadership cohort's diagnosis of the crisis of survival and proposals for response.

Much earlier, in the immediate aftermath of the Second World War and its terrifying last act—the dropping of atomic bombs on Hiroshima and Nagasaki—a small but vigorous world-order movement arose in the United States under the name of *United World Federalists*. Its impetus came from the appearance of nuclear weapons, on the one hand, and, on the other, from the failure of the governments that formed the United Nations organization in San Francisco in 1945 to place such limits on nation-state sovereignty as would make effective international peacekeeping practicable under the new world organiza-

33. Falk, *Future Worlds*, pp. 294–95 and chap. 4. For a summary of this plan, see Robert C. Johansen, *The National Interest and the Human Interest: An Analysis of U.S. Foreign Policy* (Princeton: Princeton University Press, 1980), pp. 31–36.

tion's aegis. The movement's chief initiator and first president was Cord Meyer, Jr., a serviceman who had been grievously wounded in action in the war. He diagnosed the continuing lack of enforceable world order as a deadly danger to mankind and advanced a "plan for survival" through a revision of the United Nations charter that would give it the right "to prohibit the use of force by national governments in their relations with each other."[34] In its heyday, in 1947–1948, the United World Federalists had a dues-paying membership of fifty thousand, considerable support in Congress, and help from such prominent figures as Einstein. There was also no little opposition, and Stalin's Soviet Union showed implacable hostility toward the idea of world federalism. The movement finally faded as the advent of the Cold War made the prospects for realizing its plan seem quite remote.[35]

At present, although the circumstances that underlay the rise of the United World Federalists have grown far more threatening and become entangled with the other ominous trends touched upon above, a worldwide movement under nonconstituted leadership to deal actively with the situation is notably lacking. We see the appearance of environmental movements in some countries, the organizing of numerous small-scale group efforts for monitoring world trends, arresting population growth, engaging in peace research, and designing world-order models—and little more. Explanations for this are not hard to suggest. Those already deeply afflicted by the effects of the advancing crisis, including the quarter of mankind suffering from starvation or severe malnutrition,

34. Cord Meyer, Jr., *Peace or Anarchy* (Boston: Little Brown, 1947), p. 155.
35. My account of the movement follows that given by Cord Meyer in *Facing Reality: From World Federalism to the CIA* (New York: Harper & Row, 1980), pp. 37–57.

are generally inarticulate, demoralized, desperate, unreachable by the party of humanity, and unable in any event to take active part in a movement to counteract ills of which they are earlier victims. On the other hand, those who *are* accessible to the party's diagnoses and proposals are generally people living relatively comfortable lives and hence not motivated to respond actively unless through moral concern. To this must be added the bar to a movement response in certain developed countries with authoritarian regimes that use control of the communications media to block free public discussion of the *problématique humaine*. Contemporary Soviet Russia is an example.

Still another consideration is the enormous complexity of the situation that the party of humanity seeks to diagnose, the insidiousness of the crisis, and the lack of any simple dramatic set of proposals that could furnish guidelines for a movement. In the latter connection, we have only to think back to Dr. Townsend's simple scheme for meeting the situation of the destitute elderly in depression-ridden America, or to the World Federalists' plan for transforming the United Nations by a change of its charter, to realize how much the rise of a vigorous movement may depend upon the leadership's ability to provide concrete guidelines for collective action. Even when a goal can be specified in clear, general terms, as in the concept of an ecological "steady state," the strategy of transition from continuing undifferentiated growth to the desirable future condition has not been, and cannot easily be, so formulated as to give movement activists a concrete plan of action. Nor is there any simple path of transition to a system of central guidance in world affairs.

These difficulties combine with a further obstacle to the rise of a strong movement: the persisting commitment of national governments to sovereign independence despite their inability to resolve on their own the problems that increasingly beset their nations. This goes along with the continued rootedness of the mass of men in political cultures that look to the leaderships of the nation-states as forces with the capacity to handle critical problems. Although that capacity still exists to some extent, it is limited and diminishing. But so long as the illusion prevails that the nation-states are adequate in terms of leadership competence, transition to the "organized world of tomorrow" will remain a forlorn hope. The illusion, in turn, has a deep source in the absence of a world society.

Toward Specieshood

"True leaders," according to Erikson, "create significant solidarities."[36] He has shown keen interest in how and why they do it. His Martin Luther is a man of Christendom who, by constructively overcoming a crisis of personal identity in his youth, led very many others in the same direction during a time of widespread "identity vacuum" in Europe. His Thomas Jefferson is one who, by helping to form a new and more inclusive national identity in America, had something to teach about what it might mean to form a "worldwide new identity" in our time. His Gandhi is one who, in the middle span of life, when a man or a woman may show the strength of "generativity" by defining "what and whom they have come to care for, what they care to do well, and how they plan to take care of what they have started and created," found a way of opposing others unhatingly and effecting change undestructively through nonviolent action inspired by "militant recognition of a common humanity."[37]

36. Erik H. Erikson, *Identity: Youth and Crisis* (New York: W. W. Norton, 1968), p. 191.
37. Erik H. Erikson, *Young Man Luther: A Study in Psychoanalysis*

Through his explorations of constructive leadership via identity creation and taking care, and also of the genocidally destructive leadership that can result from a pathological solution of the identity problem,[38] Erikson has employed the study of leadership as a way of *being* a leader (nonconstituted of course) who seeks to "take care" by pointing out paths to man's survival. This is the obsessive theme of his Jefferson lectures, in which he envisages the possibility of a "self-aware, all-human identity," says that the creation of an American identity, partly through Jefferson's efforts, may well be one significant model "in our slow and zigzagging road toward the realization of specieshood," and warns that "no superorganizational remedies can work without the emergence of a new measure of man."[39] He seems to be suggesting that global political institutions, global organization of human affairs, presuppose the appearance of an all-human consciousness of kind; that the mental unification of man precedes the governmental; that world governance awaits the emergence of world society. Such a perspective reverses the commonly encountered view that political organization offers the way to world society. It is a perspective worth considering.

The barrier to realizing our specieshood, in Erikson's view, is "pseudospeciation." By this he means that

and History (New York: W. W. Norton, 1958); *Dimensions of a New Identity: The 1973 Jefferson Lectures in the Humanities* (New York: W. W. Norton, 1974), p. 114; *Gandhi's Truth: On the Origins of Militant Nonviolence* (New York: W. W. Norton, 1969), p. 395; *Life History and the Historical Moment* (New York: W. W. Norton, 1975), p. 177.

38. "The Legend of Hitler's Childhood," in Erik H. Erikson, *Childhood and Society*, 2d ed. (New York: W. W. Norton, 1950), chap. 9; and "Wholeness and Totality—A Psychiatric Contribution," in *Totalitarianism*, ed. Carl J. Friedrich (Cambridge, Mass.: Harvard University Press, 1954), chap. 9.

39. Erikson, *Dimensions of a New Identity*, pp. 44, 81, 98.

"while man is obviously one species, he appears and continues on earth split up into groups (from tribes to nations, from castes to classes, from religions to ideologies) which provide their members with a firm sense of God-given identity—and a sense of immortality."[40] Elsewhere, he refers to the various national and other pseudospecies as "mythological entities," says that each of them "makes like being the human race with a glorious and ceremonially hallowed vision of itself," and goes on, "This has offered youth, in its ideological hunger, causes to live and to die for, and has attracted its heroism and self-sacrifice in periodical wars with other pseudospecies, foreign or domestic."[41] Such thinking naturally leads him at one point to ask: "Will mankind realize that it is one species— or is it destined to remain divided into 'pseudospecies' forever playing out one (necessarily incomplete) version of mankind against all the others until, in the dubious glory of the nuclear age, one version will have the power and the luck to destroy all others just moments before it perishes itself?"[42]

In Erikson's diagnosis of the situation, man is in fact, in underlying reality, one species, but everywhere remains imprisoned in "the mentality of the pseudospecies." Leaders like Gandhi and Jefferson have set out possible guidelines for dealing with the problem, but it remains unsolved and at present poses a deadly danger of humanicide through nuclear war. The supreme task of leadership is to foster a "significant solidarity" that for the first time in history will be all-inclusive. The implication is that mankind now finds itself in a specieswide "identity crisis." By an identity crisis in an individual's life, Erikson

40. Erikson, *Life History and the Historical Moment*, p. 176.
41. Erikson, *Dimensions of a New Identity*, pp. 96–97.
42. Erikson, *Life History and the Historical Moment*, p. 47.

means a life stage in young adulthood at which a person stands at a crossroads in development. He or she may achieve the sense of wholeness, continuity with past and future, and solidarity with others that belongs to a firm psychosocial identity, or fail to do so, falling into "identity diffusion" or adopting a "negative identity." This problem being a collective phenomenon in a period of identity vacuum, our time is one of supreme challenge to identity innovation, posing the question of "what it might mean to be a human being."[43]

Erikson goes this far in conceptualizing the problem: the emergence of a world society, or an all-human significant solidarity, precedes rather than follows the institutionalizing of a universal political community. In order to achieve a world society, we must somehow transcend pseudospeciation in all its varieties. People must win through to a new sense of who and what they are, a new way of identifying themselves, a new awareness of themselves as, first of all, human beings, members of a single species. Marx, it may be noted in passing, anticipated some of this when, in his early philosophical writings, he defined man as a "species being" who was destined, when the last great violent social revolution destroyed the final form of division of humans into socioeconomic classes, to achieve oneness with himself, transcendence of historic "alienation" from himself, in a specieswide society. He optimistically underestimated, however, the tenacity of pseudospeciation, especially in modern forms of nationhood and national consciousness, and did not foresee that national social revolutions carried out in the name of socialism would produce, as they have in this century, new forms of pseudospecieshood.

How might Erikson's line of thought be pursued fur-

43. Erikson, *Dimensions of a New Identity*, p. 81, and throughout Erikson's writings for the meaning of "identity crisis."

ther? Perhaps it would be fruitful to regard the phenomenon of society formation that he calls "pseudospeciation" in a positive light rather than in the negative one suggested by *pseudo*. We would then view the pseudospecies as simply incomplete versions of the species, recognizing that no holistic human society has yet emerged despite gropings in that direction. This approach propels the process of speciation, not the "pseudo" aspect of it, to the forefront of inquiry. Insofar as we can further clarify what speciation has meant in past history, we may be able better to visualize what speciation might mean if realized on a universal scale.

Let us agree that the past and present forms of society called *mythological entities* by Erikson are just that. Such in fact is the position taken earlier in the present study, when we spoke of sociocultural systems, those complexes of real and ideal culture patterns, as being rooted in a "sustaining myth," or set of myths, which gives the people composing the societies a sense of what it means to be a member of them. The word *myth*, we noted, was not meant in a pejorative sense. Forming as it does a core element of a society's ideal culture patterns and, as such, an influence upon its real culture patterns, the mythos provides the consciousness of kind that can form people into a society even when they are territorially dispersed, like the Jews of the Diaspora whose eschatological myth of Exile and Redemption underlay Zionism as formulated in the later years of the nineteenth century in Leo Pinsker's *Auto-Emancipation* and Theodor Herzl's *Judenstaat*.[44] These instances illustrate Erikson's proposition that leaders create significant solidarities. In doing so, both Pins-

44. On the "eschatological myth of Exile and Redemption," the "Zionist mythos," and the roles of Pinsker and Herzl in developing the latter, see Ben Halpern, *The Idea of the Jewish State*, 2d ed. (Cambridge, Mass.: Harvard University Press, 1969), pp. 15–17, 23.

ker and Herzl, in different ways, performed the leadership functions of defining their dispersed community's problem situation and proposing a program of action—the Zionist project—as the response.

Each sustaining myth or myth-complex offers a community-forming conception, inspirational or heroic in character, of a collective purpose, mission, or project of great significance for those engaged in it and for the world. An image of the past, a mythic history, is integral to such a mental structure. In the sustaining mythology of Afrikanerdom, for example, the Afrikaners' Great Trek into the hinterland is an important historical element.[45] But the future orientation, the conception of group mission or destiny, lies at the heart of the phenomenon. In the church-state civilizations of medieval times, the sustaining mythologies cast society as a community of believers dedicated to salvation in an afterlife. The secularization of salvation in modern mythologies of the collective project is an oft-told story, as is the rise of nationalist mythologies in recent centuries. What Columbus really discovered on these shores, it has been said, was "a new world of the mind." America emerged as the conception of a new beginning and opportunity, "the mythology of a unique nation in a New World."[46] In Leninist ideology, Soviet Russia is a federation of peoples united in belief and action and dedicated to realizing a collective mission of supreme significance in world history: the creation over time of a fully Communist society.

A society fundamentally *is* the mental structure ex-

45. For this sustaining mythology, described as a "civil religion," see T. Dunbar Moodie, *The Rise of Afrikanerdom: Power, Apartheid, and the Afrikaner Civil Religion* (Berkeley: University of California Press, 1975).

46. James Oliver Robertson, *American Myth, American Reality* (New York: Hill & Wang, 1980), pp. 28–29, 42.

pressed in a sustaining myth or myth-complex. The word *sustaining* emphasizes that people have a deep need for such myths as sustenance, in other words, a need to make their lives meaningful by being related to the lives of many others of their kind who also take part in the group's enterprise and have shared in the vicissitudes of its history. Boulding (who uses *ideology* where I speak of *mythology*) says that "an ideology must create a drama" and that its social function lies in giving the individual "a role in the drama it portrays."[47] If in the course of time a society's mythology ceases to sustain by giving its members meaningful roles to play in a valued collective enterprise, disintegrative tendencies set in. They may show up in alienation, loneliness, ennui, escape into hedonism, and receptivity to cults whose particularistic myth-structures offer sustenance that is otherwise missing in people's lives. Such phenomena, or some of them, seem to be on the increase nowadays in contemporary societies so culturally disparate as America, parts of Western Europe, and Soviet Russia.

Nevertheless, the "mythological entities," nations in particular, are far from played out as forms of social existence. The sets of myths that transform collectivities of people into societies continue, by and large, to perform that function. This being so, "pseudospeciation" can only be transcended by speciation itself, the rise and spread of a planetary consciousness resting upon a wider, nonexclusionary conception of the human project, in other words, a new, universalistic sustaining myth. An emergent world society associated with such a new mental structure could not, at least for a very long time, be anything other than a society of societies. Human beings would not be denationalized in the process of becoming

47. Boulding, *The Meaning of the Twentieth Century*, p. 162.

members of world society. From earlier, incomplete forms of speciation, however, the negativity, the "anti" elements in group identities, would be canceled in a capacious acceptance of all men and women as passengers on spaceship earth. Speaking in Hegelian dialectical terms, the rise of the new society would be the negation of the negation: earlier societies would be preserved while being transcended in the higher synthesis.

Such a change could only occur at a time when earlier, parochial sustaining myths were losing some of their hold upon many minds, especially younger ones. Teilhard de Chardin diagnosed the situation in such terms when he wrote, more than two decades ago, that, despite all appearances,

> Mankind is bored. Perhaps this is the underlying cause of all our troubles. We no longer know what to do with ourselves. Hence in social terms the disorderly turmoil of individuals pursuing conflicting and egoistical aims; and, on the national scale, the chaos of armed conflict in which, for want of a better object, the excess of accumulated energy is destructively released.[48]

Perhaps it was the plight of mankind having become bored for lack of a sense of involvement in a worthwhile collective project that inspired Federico Fellini's film *Eight and a Half*, whose portrait of a film company with cameramen and actors all ready, but frustrated for lack of a script or plot, might have been intended to symbolize mankind in search of a reason for its existence on earth. If we take seriously the idea that a sustaining myth involves a drama in which people all have meaningful parts to play, then we might look rather to artists than to natural

48. Pierre Teilhard de Chardin, *The Future of Man*, trans. Norman Denny (New York: Harper & Row, 1964), p. 151. The book originally was published in France in 1959.

or social scientists for the act of social script-production of which, like Fellini's would-be filmmakers, we stand in need.

Teilhard de Chardin thought he discerned, especially among such groups as scientists, thinkers, and airmen, the appearance of a new kind of person, "*Homo progressivus*, that is to say, the man to whom the terrestrial future matters more than the present."[49] Whether he was right or wrong about that, the theme of concern for the terrestrial future has been sounded again and again by spokesmen of the party of humanity. It underscores the urgency of a new existential awareness characterized by care for the far future. Even if we take this to mean the human future, that is necessarily bound up with the preservation of other forms of life that make the earth a viable habitat for man. Moral responsibility for the future involves a radical mutation in what has been the normal human outlook up to now. "The earth, infinite in its bounty, is at our disposal," has been the implicit motto, and concern for those who will live a thousand or ten thousand generations from now has been absent. As a moral party, our leadership cohort would change that.

Mankind at the Turning Point puts the argument for a future orientation on practical grounds: "If the human species is to survive, man must develop *a sense of identification with future generations* and be ready to trade benefits to the next generations for the benefits to itself. If each generation aims at maximum good for itself, *Homo Sapiens* is doomed."[50] While not easily answerable, this line of argument strikes me as weak because it fails to

49. Ibid., p. 142.

50. Mesarovic and Pestel, *Mankind at the Turning Point*, p. 147. In *Civilization in Crisis: Human Prospects in a Changing World* (Cambridge: Cambridge University Press, 1976), pp. 221–22, Joseph A. Camilleri deplores the "obsessive preoccupation with the present" and

acknowledge that the issue is fundamentally ethical, a question of values, and not—or not only—a matter of trade-offs between generations. Why, after all, should we be "right-to-lifers" for generations a million years away? Why should it be a matter of concern to a living generation engaged in despoiling the earth and squandering its resources if *Homo sapiens* is doomed as a consequence? Why should even the ethics of reverence for life extend to life in an indefinitely prolonged future?

A part of the answer might be that immortality for the species is the one form of immortality that man has the power, apart from cosmic cataclysm, to ensure, and immortality is a universal value. There are reinforcing considerations, again ethical. Whatever our religious beliefs or doubts, we have a past to keep faith with and to keep alive, so that the cultural creations of man will remain available for future humans to contemplate and appreciate. It is notable that we can most easily ignore the negativities of incomplete speciation in our consciousness of the past; there, the exclusionary aspects of collective identities cease to be divisive, they fade in importance. We need not be Greeks to take pride in the Parthenon, or Germans to love Beethoven. From this point of view, the mission of man on earth could be seen as one not only of stewardship (a term used by one of the writers cited earlier), but also of custodianship. Custodianship of the memory of the past, of history as the reconstruction of what happened and why, of culture as the accumulated creations of the past, of the potentiality of further culture

---

"the addictive habit of discounting the future, of attributing priority to short-term parochial interests, especially apparent in the modern state's economic and defense policies, which merely serves to hasten the arrival of the future and to compound the difficulties it poses for the present."

creation, and of the possibility of future inklings into the still unsolved mystery of being.

Such an answer is not likely to satisfy more than the relatively few engaged in such pursuits, however, and we are left in the end with a void that can only be filled by visionary minds capable of innovating a powerfully persuasive, universalistic conception of the human project as the basis for the set of values that will be needed if civilization is to be placed in a steady state and specieshood realized. Of such creation of significant solidarity on a global scale we so far see little sign. Yet it is possible to envisage what an "all-human identity" might entail by reliving one person's experience of breaking through to planetary consciousness.

So far, twelve men have stood on the moon. The first were Neil Armstrong and Colonel Edwin Aldrin. On 20 July 1969, they descended toward the lunar surface in a craft called the Eagle. On the approach they discovered that what our maps euphemistically called the Sea of Tranquillity is strewn with boulders and that the dust stirred up by the Eagle's rockets kept them from making out what might be a safe place to come down. The NASA space center on earth considered the possibility of aborting the mission but decided to let it go forward, and the craft landed on a smooth spot. The two men climbed down a ladder, stepped onto the lunar soil, walked around, gathered specimens of lunar rock, planted an American flag, and saluted it. But most of all, they looked at the earth.

Armstrong was interviewed for the tenth anniversary of the event. When asked how he felt as he saluted the flag, he answered: "I suppose you're thinking about pride and patriotism. But we didn't have a strong nationalistic feeling at that time. We felt more that it was a venture of all mankind and we were delighted to be a part of the country that made it happen." Had he spoken in Erikson's terminology, he might have explained that he hadn't lost his sense of American identity but that it had been over-laid by a new sense of wholeness, an awareness of kinship with all the people on a heavenly body where the dividing lines between sovereign nation-states were invisible.

But his own account tells it best: "There's one sight I'll never forget. As I stood on the Sea of Tranquillity and looked up at the earth, my impression was of the impor-tance of that small, fragile, remote blue planet. People everywhere have, by television and photographs, shared that perspective and shared our concern for the security of our globe."[51]

A Platonic Conclusion

Having begun this little book with a thesis from Plato, we may fittingly consult him again at the end. Liv-ing in so different a world so long ago, he could not have foreseen the crisis of survival that has emerged in the twentieth century. But if he had been given a preview of future history up to now, he would not have been greatly surprised to learn that humanity would get into deep trouble, becoming a species mortally dangerous to itself. Knowing how rare true *politiké* was then, he could hardly have expected it to grow common later on. So, in his great work, *The Republic*, he designed an ideal polity characterized by the rule of reason over the warlike spirit and the gross appetites of people and envisioned its real-ization on condition of "philosophy" coming to power. That, his Socrates suggested, could happen in one of two

51. *The New York Times*, 20 July 1979.

different ways: either philosophers might be compelled, whether they willed or not, to "take care of the state," or else kings or princes themselves might become "divinely inspired by a true love of true philosophy." There was no impossibility in all this, but "that there is a difficulty, we acknowledge ourselves."[52]

The relevance of Plato's thought to our present set of problems may seem remote. The party of humanity, if we may take its thinking as the contemporary embodiment of "philosophy," is not seeking to design an ideal polity but to keep a world afloat at a time when there is no political leadership of the whole and leadership of separate parts for their own sakes does and will, in certain ways, defeat elementary requirements of leadership of the whole. Furthermore, the continuing absence of a vigorous world-wide movement under nonconstituted leadership is evidence, if such were needed, that "philosophy" is not going to be compelled to "take care of the state." Nowhere do we see such philosophers becoming kings, presidents, or general secretaries, or the likelihood that they will. Meanwhile, the spaceship is adrift unpiloted, and the passengers in different sections are not sufficiently aware of themselves as a totality to permit a central guidance system to emerge.

This leaves open one possibility. It is slim, but we are not now in a position to dismiss any possibility on that account. "Philosophy," as currently embodied in the party of humanity's thinking, does not seem destined for kingship, and kingship in the hundred and fifty or so existing nation-states gives no indication of becoming "divinely inspired by a true love of true philosophy." There are, however, a small number of great states whose aggregate size, population, power, wealth, and resources give them the

52. *The Dialogues of Plato*, trans. B. Jowett, 1: 760.

capacity to provide *interim* leadership of the whole if their constituted political authorities should define the global situation in its true dimensions of crisis, devise a set of appropriate responses, and then employ, in combination, their mighty separate abilities to mobilize requisite support both within their own political communities and among the governments of the large number of other states and *their* political communities. Among these great states with the capacity to exert decisive influence if they act in combination, the United States and Russia stand out as potential candidates for the interim-leadership role by virtue of their superpower status and because their mutual relationships have so far been constructed on an adversary basis with a very limited cooperative element that, as argued above, is periodically and predictably endangered by tensions and confrontations generated by their competition for influence around the world. To this we might add their competition for primacy, or parity plus, in strategic power for potential use against one another. Should their competitive relationship undergo basic change through a deliberate decision by the leaderships on both sides, the political condition of the world would be transformed.

So far two different versions of a radically new superpower relationship have been bruited. One is the model of a collusive Russo-American "condominium." This would be a political counterpart of the situation of duopoly in economics, where two giant firms jointly dominate the market and act in their concerted individual interests. Curbing their influence rivalry, the two superpowers would use their combined force and influence to impose their wills on all other states with the aim of establishing and maintaining a mutually acceptable world order that would serve their respective interests *as superpowers*. Probably such a world order would witness a division of the globe into two huge spheres of influence, reproducing on a vastly enlarged scale the Soviet-German division of Eastern Europe and the Balkans into spheres of influence in 1939.

Because this is a power approach in essence and not a leadership approach, and because it would be inspired not by "philosophy" as interpreted here but rather by the conventionally conceived self-interests of the colluding superpowers, it does not correspond to the meaning of a Platonic interim-leadership strategy. It would completely miss Plato's central point: that the constituted leader or leaders of an existing state might undergo a conversion to a new way of understanding that would result in a rule of reason, an order embodying *politiké*. Moreover, such a power solution would face a number of extremely serious practical difficulties. It would be beset, in particular, by manifold resistances from smaller states whose interests were being overridden by the superpowers.[53]

The alternative version, which would correspond to the meaning of a Platonic transition strategy, envisages a cooperative arrangement open to all other governments to join. Indeed, as a leadership approach it would necessarily involve rational persuasion in the superpowers' combined efforts to mobilize the support of other governments for their definition of man's situation and their projects for responses by governments and peoples. Hospitality to the thinking of other constituted and non-constituted leaderships, and concern for the interests of all, would be in the spirit of such an approach. The two superpowers would simply be doing what leaders, by

53. Robert C. Tucker, "United States–Soviet Cooperation: Incentives and Obstacles," *The Annals of the American Academy of Political and Social Science* 372 (July 1967): 11. For detailed discussion and a trenchant critique of the condominium model, see Falk, *Future Worlds*, pp. 206–9.

definition, do, that is, *taking the lead*, in this instance the lead in what Plato (anticipating Erikson) called taking care of the state—the state now conceived in global terms.

Under such a Russo-American entente for human survival, the two governments, instead of cooperating politically in their own national interests narrowly conceived, would exert their influence separately and jointly on behalf of order and the arresting of the further growth of the crisis syndrome. This is in the interest not simply of these two major nations but of all. They would work not only in their bilateral relations but also in the United Nations and its working bodies, in their regional alliances, and in every aspect of foreign and domestic policy to promote constructive change and peaceful solutions of world problems. In effect, the Russo-American entente would become a kind of trusteeship under which the two governments would jointly act as sponsors of international order pending the creation of a workable formal system of order. It would be a holding operation to help man survive long enough to develop the world society that is needed but does not yet exist.[54]

Such a project has taken shape in some Russian as well as some American minds. The memorandum by Andrei Sakharov on "Progress, Coexistence, and Intellectual Freedom" called for recognition of the nature of the world crisis and, in response, all-round cooperation between the United States and Russia. What it envisaged was not a condominium, not a collusion of the superpowers behind the rest of the world's back, but an open collaboration for humanity's sake, a joining of minds and energies of two great nations in pursuit of peace and the solution of in-

54. In this paragraph I have drawn upon a passage from pp. 11–12 of the article cited in the previous note.

creasingly urgent world problems. This program was linked with the prospect of gradual convergence between the two systems of society and in particular with progress toward a greatly liberalized, in fact open, society in Russia.[55]

Sakharov is not alone among Russians in taking so serious a view of the situation and envisaging a Russo-American entente. A voice from within the Soviet establishment spoke out along similar lines in another memorandum that circulated informally inside Russia and eventually made its way abroad. The memorandum began as follows:

> The atomic death threatening mankind can be averted only on condition of an alliance of unity between the great nuclear powers of the world—Russia and the United States. Only the creation of such an alliance can lead to real disarmament and the creation of the single system of free states absolutely necessary for our planet, the gradual overcoming of the most dangerous contradictions of the present period: between the world character of production and the nation-state (with some regional adjustment) form of economic life, between the developed countries with high levels of consumption and the remaining countries with low levels of consumption. In a word, only this alliance can inaugurate a harmonious development of the world and ensure the natural and progressive development of this process that is vitally necessary to humanity.[56]

The author proceeded to argue in the remainder of the memorandum that the necessary alliance would not be

55. The memorandum appears in *Sakharov Speaks*, ed. Harrison E. Salisbury (New York: Vintage Books, 1974), pp. 55–114. The first line epitomizes Sakharov's definition of the situation: "The division of mankind threatens it with destruction."

56. The memorandum, signed Fedor Zniakov (which may be a pseudonym) and dated May 1966, is available in American libraries in *Arkhiv samizdata*, document no. 374, in Russian.

realizable without a fundamental reform of the "super-monopolistic organization of society" in Soviet Russia.

That was 1966. No such reform has occurred in the intervening years, and none seems in prospect at present. Russian proponents of it nevertheless remain convinced, rightly so in my view, that it is vitally needed. In a restatement of his credo that Sakharov has managed to send out from his apartment-prison in Gorky, we read: "A most important thesis that in the course of time became the foundation of my position is the inseparable link between international security and international trust, on the one hand, and respect for human rights, the openness of society, on the other."[57] Without a Russian renewal, whereby that country's society comes to public life in ways no longer trammeled by a political system responsive only to the narrowly self-centered concerns of the super-monopoly, Russia cannot play a constructive role of world leadership commensurate with the humane and universalistic values by which her best sons and daughters, past and present, have lived.

Consequently, as 1980 ends, the obstacles to a Russo-American entente for human survival are so formidable that the project may appear quite utopian. Not only do present internal conditions in Russia preclude it. Deep changes in the American leadership psyche, public attitudes, and ways of living would also be needed. Nor is there any guarantee that if conditions in both countries should undergo change in the directions indicated, a leadership alliance between the two for world peace and order would materialize. Such great and powerful

57. Academician Andrei Sakharov, "Open Letter to the President of the Academy of Sciences of the USSR, A. P. Aleksandrov," *Novoye Russkoye Slovo*, 14 December 1980. The open letter is dated 20 October 1980. *Novoye Russkoye Slovo* is a Russian-language daily paper published in New York.

nation-states could go on acting in the ways that nation-states have acted in the past. That could well happen. But it is not inevitable that it should happen—not, at any rate, if the argument advanced in this book has merit. The leadership approach to politics is one that takes human freedom seriously. It holds that human beings and their leaders have the capacity to learn from history and past mistakes, to take accurate measure of present situations, and to take action inspired by a sense of the common good.

Never—to paraphrase Lincoln's words cited earlier—have the dogmas of the quiet past been so fearfully inadequate to the stormy and ominous present. Never has the human occasion been piled so high with awful difficulty. Never has it been so urgently requisite to think and act anew, because never have the people—all of them—been confronted by a case so radically new. Leadership must diagnose the situation and devise the courses of action that are needed to meet it. That it will be difficult no one can deny. But in the face of this difficulty, a member of the party of humanity can only say with Jean Monnet: "If action is necessary, how can one say that it is impossible, so long as one has not tried it?"

Afterword

Robert C. Tucker's *Politics as Leadership* was originally presented at the University of Missouri–Columbia in the form of three public lectures on April 10 and 11, 1980. These lectures were the eleventh of the Paul Anthony Brick Lectures, a series of commentaries on various aspects of the "science of ethics" made possible by the bequest of Paul Anthony Brick, a citizen of Missouri at the time of his death.

The first Brick Lectures, *Morals for Mankind*, were delivered in 1960 by Herbert W. Schneider, professor emeritus of philosophy at Columbia University, and published by the University of Missouri Press the following year. Subsequent titles in the series, all of them similarly published, are *The Three Worlds of Man*, 1962, by Stringfellow Barr, educator, author, and editor; *The Reluctant Revolutionary*, 1963, by Edward Teller, physicist and recipient of the Albert Einstein Medal for 1959; *The Ethics of United States Foreign Relations*, 1964, by Erwin D. Canham, editor-in-chief of *The Christian Science Monitor*; *The Man in the Middle*, 1965, by Harry S. Ashmore, recipient of the Pulitzer Prize in Journalism for 1958 as editor of the *Little Rock Arkansas Gazette*, which was also awarded a Pulitzer Prize; *The Persistent Quest for Values: What Are We Seeking?*, 1966, by Harlan Hatcher, president of The University of Michigan; *Human Nature in American Historical Thought*, 1966, by Merle Curti, Frederick Jackson Turner Professor of History, The University of Wisconsin; and *The Hero and the Blues*, 1972, by Albert Murray, author and educator. The eighth lectures in the Brick Series, presented by Abraham Kaplan in 1970, and the tenth, presented by Paul Ricoeur in 1977, have not yet been published.

Edward D. King
Director, University of Missouri Press

Index

Index

Index